UNDRAFTED and PURPOSED

Still Living, Loving, and Leading in Life

Kervin K. Searles, LPC

ISBN: 979-8-9931235-1-6 (Paperback)

ISBN: 979-8-9931235-0-9 (Hardcover)

ISBN: 979-8-9931235-2-3 (eBook)

Book design by Dara Publishing LLC

Place of Publication: Greenwood, South Carolina, 29646

Library of Congress: 2025919738

Printed in the United States of America.

Disclaimer: The publisher and the author do not make any guarantee or other promise as to any results that may be obtained from using the content of this book. This publication is meant as a source of valuable information for the reader. However, it is not a substitute for direct expert assistance. If such a level of assistance is required, the services of a competent professional should be sought.

Dedication

This book is dedicated to my dad who was once a man who was once a boy.

TABLE OF CONTENTS

PREFACE

I began writing this book earlier this year, in January (2025). I had a clear purpose in mind and that was to reach men beyond a classroom and therapy office. I aimed to offer them tools to better understand themselves, their emotions, and the effects, both great and small, that they create in their families and communities.

For years, I have sat with men in honest and raw conversations about anger, relationships, and the hidden burdens they carry. I have watched men wrestle with traumas that are handed down through generations also known as intergenerational trauma. I have seen how these struggles show up in behaviors that hurt them and the people they love. I wanted to put all of this into something men could carry with them long after our sessions ended. This includes the insights, the lessons, the stories, and the theories that guide my practice.

Like a coach preparing his players for game day, I wrote this book to help men understand the plays they've been running, some instinctual, some inherited, and to offer a clearer strategy for leading themselves, their families, and their communities with intention. This is the strategy I would offer to any man who is serious about winning in the game of life and reaching his full potential.

This book weaves together personal experiences, Adlerian principles, well-known truths, and research-based techniques. My hope is that it will spark a shift. I want men who read these pages to begin seeing themselves not only as performers but also as sons, brothers, uncles, fathers, and individuals who are also leaders. These men will shape the health and resilience of their families and communities for generations to come.

The journey of writing these words was not easy. Between January and August 2, 2025, my family faced several major illnesses and surgeries. These were relatives I love deeply, and being there for them meant stepping away from writing, stepping away from work, and showing up in the way a man should for his family. Those moments tested my commitment while deepening my purpose. They reminded me that true leadership is strengthened by tough experiences, not by comfort.

Along the way, I also realized that completing this book was proof that I can accomplish anything I set my mind to and that I do not need to wait for permission to share what I know. I wrote these pages to invest in you as the reader, and by doing so, I invested in myself. Along the way, I came to understand that trials are both inevitable and necessary, because they strengthen and affirm the perspective and insight I offer you from my window of the world.

If you've ever felt undrafted, misjudged, or overlooked, this book is your playbook. These pages are meant to equip you with tools to win in life. Whether you're yearning to be noticed and appreciated or stepping more into a leadership role, the goal is not perfection but living with purpose.

May this book help you lead better, love deeper, and leave behind a legacy of strength, health, and connection.

Kervin K. Searles, LPC

INTRODUCTION

More often than not, you are seen as a performer. As a Black man in America, you are often viewed as an athlete, an entertainer, or, unfortunately, as a thug or a streetwise individual. How you fit into that mold determines whether society drafts you or discards you. This book exists to break that narrative in half.

Undrafted & Purposed is for you. A man who knows there is more to you than the labels you've been given or the opportunities you have been overlooked for. You may not have been "drafted" by society based on your current skills, but you are still purposed. You are purposed to live well, lead well, and love well.

Inside these pages, you will not find a rulebook, a lecture, or a guaranteed contract. Instead, you'll find a roadmap for self-awareness, connection, and commitment. You will explore the hidden forces that have shaped your choices. You will acknowledge your need for respect, your desire for belonging, your drive for freedom, and your requirement for control.

This book won't shy away from your truth but push you toward it. It will ask you to look at your past, not just your mistakes, burdens, and traumas, but also your successes, your roles within your family and community, and the core values that guide you.

I know what it feels like to question your worth and second-guess your value. As a therapist, a father, and a husband, I have had to deeply understand myself, my emotions, and the impact they carry in order to break the old, familiar patterns I'm now inviting you to break.

This book will challenge you to ask the right questions for honest introspection and help you focus your mind on what you can do starting today.

If you're ready to go beyond the locker room and barbershop talk and dig deeper into the reasons behind your choices, habits, and relationships, then keep reading. If you have been giving without ever receiving guidance and leading without ever being led, then this book will challenge you and encourage you at the same time.

Each page is an invitation to get honest about your story and intentional about your future. When you dig into your own motivations, you own the power to choose your next play with clarity and confidence.

Every move you make counts. Every choice builds the legacy you'll leave behind.

This book is divided into three parts, each building on the last:

Part I: Self-Awareness helps you learn about where you come from and how your past still affects your life today.

Part II: Connection looks at how your relationships with family, friends, and your community affect how you see yourself and feel like you belong.

Part III: Commitment asks you to take full responsibility for your growth and to show up as a man with clear goals, strong discipline, and lasting strength.

Each chapter is connected to a strategy in your personal game plan which guides you toward clarity, connection, and purpose.

Remember, this isn't about being perfect. It's about being purposed. Are you undrafted? Maybe. But your purpose has never really been up for discussion.

Turn the page.

PART I
SELF-AWARENESS

Before a man can grow from a boy, he must first understand himself. These first chapters focus on self-awareness and your ability to recognize how your lifestyle, habits, and mindset have been shaped by everything you have lived through. This includes your childhood experiences, past relationships, and cultural messaging. You will take a close look at your past, your patterns, and the choices you have made. This reflection is not about judgment. It is about learning and growing. Self-awareness helps you connect the dots and begin making intentional choices that align with who you are becoming.

CHAPTER 1

GAME PLAN

REALIZING YOUR UNIQUE LIFESTYLE

Unexpected Birth

I was supposed to be aborted. But I wasn't.

That thought has lived in the back of my mind for as long as I can remember. It was something my mother told me during one of my early years in an effort to enlighten me about my unique abilities. She shared this truth not to harm, but to explain, to clarify, to connect. The story didn't come with bitterness or regret, but with honesty and a sense of intrigue. From the beginning, I came to understand it not as a rejection, but as something that gave my life a unique kind of meaning.

At the time of my conception, my parents were young. They had recently married and had already welcomed my older brother into the world. Both of them were barely into adulthood and still trying to find their way in life. They had low income, limited savings, and very little work experience. I imagine their life was filled with uncertainty and worry. The idea of bringing another child into that situation may have felt overwhelming. They were not hardened or heartless, they were scared. Raising two children during a time in the 1970s of high inflation and high unemployment would have required a lot of support from their families already strained across the country. After much discussion, they made a decision. They found an address for a clinic in the next city over and set out with the intention of ending the pregnancy. It wasn't something they took lightly. It was a decision born out of fear and practicality. However, as they drove, something unexpected happened. They got lost. This was before MapQuest, GPS, and smartphones. Directions came on a printed map or instructions from someone who had previously been. My parents had only the address and no sign, no phone number, no map. They didn't even have an idea of what the place looked like. They drove around for what felt like forever, circling unfamiliar streets, growing more confused and frustrated by the minute. At some point, after what must have felt like an eternity of searching, they gave up. The place was never found. The job was left undone.

On the way home, the drive allowed for something to shift in my mother. She sat with silence as she began to feel something deeper within her, literally and figuratively. She later shared with me that she felt that I was meant to be here. She didn't know how or why, but she believed that something special would come from me. When I first heard this story as a child, I didn't fully understand the weight of it. But I also didn't meet it with a lens of abandonment or rejection. I didn't focus on the fact that my parents almost chose not to have me. Instead, I took it as evidence that something bigger was at play in my life. Of course, some people might hear this story and interpret it differently. You might focus on the fact that I was nearly erased before I had a name. Or think, "She didn't really want you." Another thought could be, "Why even share that with a child?" I am not sure if there is a specific timeline that you could deem appropriate for sharing this story with a child. But even as I received the message, I was developing how I chose to understand it and the world. And that perspective makes all the difference.

Please understand that you experience life through the meanings you give the moments that shape you. The same event can break one person and empower another, depending entirely on how it's interpreted. And for me, this story became the foundation of my sense of self and my perception of the world. I decided early on that it wasn't just happenstance that I was here but I was chosen by something greater. That perspective gave me resilience. It gave me a sense of direction even when I didn't always know where I was going. It reminded me that I was special, even when life felt uncertain or overwhelming. The story of my almost-abortion isn't something I carry with shame. It's not a secret I try to bury. It's something I honor, because it reminds me that life is fragile and full of turning points, many of which are beyond our control. But even in that fragility, meaning can be found. I think about the randomness of that day. If they had taken one different turn, if they had asked the right person for directions, if they had searched for the clinic just five more minutes, maybe I wouldn't be here writing this. Maybe none of what I've done in my life would have happened. But they didn't. They got lost and stayed lost. And in that loss, I was given a chance. And that's how I've chosen to live—not as someone unwanted, but as someone spared, preserved, and placed here for a reason. My story didn't begin with certainty, but it began with enough. Enough love, enough hope, and enough chance for something new to grow.

You have stories like this and moments (or plays) that define you. These plays send messages to your brain that help shape your identity or push you to behave in ways that are a defense mechanism for protection of your peace. But you don't have to keep running the same plays. You are not locked into one specific game plan. Every day gives you the opportunity to call a new play, to make a new choice and live from a deeper truth. Your lifestyle is your personal philosophy that is a living, breathing strategy for how you carry your name, your purpose, and your story into the world. And the most powerful part? You get to revise it. Not to erase what you've been through, but to build on it with clarity, with intention, and with truth. You've already been writing your playbook. Now it's time to read it. Understand it. And, if necessary, rewrite it.

This chapter is about understanding lifestyle as a man's identity in motion. I want to help you see how your choices, pain, and patterns form the life you live and how you can begin to revise it with intention.

Unexpected Death (A Father's Influence and Legacy)

March 4, 2000. Twenty-three years after my unexpected birth. On this day, I began to understand the purpose and meaning connected with the lifestyle of a man. My father was forty-three years old. He seemingly lived a life rich with purpose. His moves were guided by personal choice, routine, and deeply held values. I will forever remember how he carried the weight of daily problems, how he loved, and how he showed up for me and others without losing sight of himself.

He grew up in a small town, the baby of the family in a two-parent household. That upbringing, whether good, bad, or indifferent, gave him his first sense of the meaning of life. He made some good choices. He made some bad ones too. But each choice left a mark on him, the man he became, and subsequently the man I would become as one of his children. Over time, his experiences shaped a lifestyle that wasn't just about surviving but thriving and living the optimal life based on the hand he was dealt. He developed routines grounded in his beliefs and placed God first, my mom second, children third, and then everything else. That order rarely shifted, if ever, and yet he made no one feel less than or after the other.

My dad was my first blueprint of manhood. Growing up, the simplest statements from others connected me with my dad. Statements such as, "You have dimples like your dad," or "You're always smiling like your father." These statements, as simple as they were, connected positive perceptions on masculinity and laid the foundation for what I saw as a man. As I got older, those comments changed and other people would suggest that I would one day grow into the same cool, smooth, godly type of man he became in his later years. Those years continued to groom him into a man comfortable in his skin, confident without arrogance, grounded in who he was and a servant of the Most High.

When he passed, I experienced so much grief. The first two years were the hardest. That grief followed me everywhere I went, as I relearned life without him. He was supposed to be the best man at my wedding because I felt he taught me what it looked like to love deeply. Additionally, he worked with integrity, moved with grace, and always showed kindness. Whether he was working in the church or spending time with his family, he carried himself with a wisdom and faith that was unwavering. If he was tired, we didn't know it. If he was struggling, we didn't feel it. Because in every moment, he was fully present. In his absence, his lifestyle has lived on in the choices I have made in recent years.

In retrospect, the experience of my unexpected birth and his early death led me to a unique perspective and understanding of life. I came to realize that regardless of its length, it can be both meaningful and impactful when it is lived with purpose. Although my dad lived a few short years, I was privileged to spend twenty-three of those years as his son. In that time, I witnessed a life marked by intention, discipline, and love. His journey affirmed for me that what matters most is how one chooses to live. In my father's case, it seemed his sense of purpose was closely tied to his values and daily routine. He defined success by his ability to create, develop, and support his family. His routine reflected his priorities that I outlined earlier: God first, my mother second, children third, and then everything else. That structure, grounded in his beliefs, never made anyone feel forgotten or misplaced; instead, it offered our family both stability and clarity.

Through his example, I learned that manhood is much more than physical strength or social status. True masculinity was about being present, responsible, and emotionally available. He loved my mother deeply and subsequently his children whom they came together to make. He also worked diligently, sharing his faith in God as he moved through life. His character taught me that being a man means showing up not just physically, but emotionally and spiritually for the people who count on you. I also realized that his choices, both good and bad, shaped the legacy he left behind. Every decision he made left an imprint not only on his own life, but on mine, and now on my children as well. His life reminded me that one is a sum of the choices they make, and those choices ripple far beyond them. Whether you are building a life of intention or reacting out of pain, you are laying the foundation for what others will one day remember. Even in times of struggle, my father remained emotionally available and steady. He never allowed his hardships to overshadow his presence. That quiet strength and the ability to remain consistent even in difficulty was one of his greatest attributes. He showed me that resilience is not about hiding weakness but about staying grounded in the face of adversity.

Perhaps most importantly, I came to understand that legacy is carried out through lifestyle. My father is remembered not for grand gestures or public achievements, but for the way he lived each day. The way he treated people. The way he honored his commitments. The way he remained true to who he was. In the end, his example reflected that your consistent actions more than your intentions or occasional efforts shape how you are remembered. His life was purposeful and from his example, I have learned to strive for a life that is just the same.

Personal Reflection and Early Adulthood

In reflecting on my father's life, I've come to believe that his lifestyle was shaped by a clear, internal goal that was never stated aloud. Though I can no longer ask him directly, the choices he made and the way he carried himself provided strong clues. By comparing his lifestyle to mine and many others like me, it becomes clear that your way of living is never random but rather it is deliberate, evolving, and deeply personal.

Lifestyle can be understood as your identity in motion. It is a working document that is constantly revised, restructured, and redefined from one milestone to the next. Rather than being fixed or final, your lifestyle is who you are. It is shaped by ongoing experiences, the decisions you make, the relationships you build, and the challenges you overcome.

For example, choosing to pursue higher education or take a job after high school can shift your priorities and sense of responsibility. Ending a difficult relationship or building a network of friends can influence how you connect with others and how you go after what you want. Overcoming financial hardship or navigating grief can deepen your resilience. Each of these moments contributes to your style of life and to who you are becoming. From early childhood memories to the daily choices of adulthood, you are in a constant state of becoming. Each stage of life brings new insights that shape how you think, feel, and behave. The way you live out that identity evolves even as the core you formed in childhood remains.

From childhood, the foundation of your lifestyle begins to take shape. The family environment you grow up in, the lessons you are taught, and the relationships you form early on help define how you see the world.

Let's take a simple example. Imagine you are often told that you are a good singer. The praise encourages you, so you sing more. Throughout your childhood, your experiences of singing with others confirm what you have heard: you are better than most boys your age. You enjoy the recognition and begin to dream about becoming a singer. But as you grow older, you come face to face with reality. You learn that you can hold a note but do not have the kind of talent to make a career of it. Eventually, you decide to stop pursuing singing. That decision is not random. It is shaped by what you have heard, what you have learned, and how you have felt throughout your life. Your opinion of yourself shifts, and your behavior follows.

Various influences shape your expectations in life. They also affect how you respond to conflict. For example, if you were raised in a home where anger was met with silence, you may have learned to shut down during arguments. These influences play a role in forming your patterns of attachment, such as expecting your partner to remain quiet even in anger because of what you learned about anger in your childhood. Even as you mature, the experiences you gather continue to shape your inner framework. You collect these experiences over time through interactions at school with teachers and friends, as well as at home and in your neighborhood—essentially, wherever you go before reaching adulthood.

What you value, how you respond to challenges, how you relate to others, and how you care for yourself all become key plays in the personal game plan of your lifestyle. Every decision adds to your strategy. Your habits form the daily drills, your relationships act as teammates, and your values serve as the playbook that guides each move. Over time, these elements shape how you show up in the game of life. The way you live is not just a reflection of who you were. It is also a reflection of who you are choosing to become, moment by moment.

Living by Design, Not by Default

Ultimately, your lifestyle is your personal narrative in motion. It is constantly updated by your self-reflection, your intentional growth, and your courage to reimagine what is possible. It is a record of beliefs you have questioned, habits you have refined, and behaviors you have reshaped to align with deeper awareness. No two lifestyles are identical because no two lives are identical. You carry your own unique blend of history, experiences, and choices, and they continue to shape how you move through the world.

When you see your lifestyle in this way, you can approach it with both grace and curiosity. Grace allows you to honor your past and the lessons it has given you. Curiosity pushes you to explore what is next. This mindset gives you the power to be both author and editor of your identity. You are not defined by one version of yourself. You are always evolving toward greater clarity, wholeness, and intention.

At the center of that evolution is the pursuit of your ultimate goal. The journey toward that goal, along with the small wins along the way, can give you a deep sense of fulfillment. You feel proud and accomplished, and you should take time to reflect on how far you have come. You enjoy the rewards of your effort and perseverance. But when things do not go as planned, it is easy to become discouraged. That discouragement can slowly turn into bitterness. If bitterness goes unchecked, it often becomes anger. In that state, your choices can turn reactive. You may start acting out of pain instead of purpose. You may try to numb the hurt or prove something to others. In chasing quick relief, you risk creating a lifestyle you never intended. A lifestyle shaped more by reaction than by intention. That is why it is crucial to build your lifestyle on conscious decisions. Your choices should reflect the life you truly want and be shaped by the lessons you have learned, not simply by emotional reactions to what you have experienced.

Every man holds a personal opinion of who he is. That opinion is not formed in isolation. It is shaped by what you hear about yourself and by what you discover through your own life experiences. By extension your choices are not just random decisions. They are reflections of how you see yourself, what you believe about your potential, and what you have chosen to accept or reject about your place in the world. Your choices are not isolated actions either. They are informed responses shaped by how you see yourself and what you believe is possible. Every day presents new decisions, and each one is filtered through your self-image, your past experiences, and the messages you have internalized from others. Over time, those repeated decisions form consistent behaviors. Those behaviors become habits. Habits develop into routines, and eventually, those routines shape the lifestyle you live.

As you live and make choices, you also form an internal compass of values. You see the results of your efforts and the impact of your decisions, and you gain clarity on what truly matters to you. Your values guide you, but your choices will either affirm them or challenge them, especially in moments when life does not go as planned. The real work is in aligning your routines with your values. That alignment will define both the lifestyle you live and the man you become.

Your lifestyle of principles, assumptions, and routines guides your every move. It is not fixed. It evolves with your experiences, your intentions, and your reflections. This is your game plan. It is the pattern of decisions, beliefs, and behaviors that shape how you move through life. Whether it comes from what you inherited in your upbringing or from choices you have made through deep reflection, your lifestyle is the strategy you live by. The advantage is that you can revise it at any time. Just as Tony Dungy was known for making defensive adjustments mid-game, you have the power to adjust your routines, change your direction, and realign your values with the way you live every day.

At its core, your lifestyle is a living philosophy. It shapes how you see the world, how you respond to it, and what you strive for within it. It is the script you write, edit, and perform daily, often without even realizing it.

PAUSE, REFLECT, AND RECLAIM

Your lifestyle is your personal philosophy, a living, breathing strategy that reflects your values, identity, and vision. You have the ability to revise it at any time. You're not locked into past decisions, old pain, or inherited patterns. You can choose differently. You can rewrite your playbook. Before you move forward, pause and reflect:

Ask Yourself:

◊   What parts of your lifestyle feel like they were inherited, not chosen?

◊ What experiences from your past have shaped how you see yourself today?

◊ What daily routines or habits do you need to realign with your true values?

Locker Room Wisdom:
"You've already been writing your playbook.
Now it's time to read it.
Understand it.
And, if necessary, rewrite it."

Let's begin with childhood.

CHAPTER 2

EARLY COACHING

CHILDHOOD EXPERIENCES

The First Inning – Childhood as Life's Warm-Up

Imagine a young kid stepping onto a baseball field for the first time. His uniform is too big for his size, his hands are unable to fit in the glove purchased by his dad, and although he is very fast, when he is running, it seems the line to first base is oh so long and he will never get there. But still he is there for the first practice, all excited and eager to meet new kids and learn this game that everyone is talking about at school. The coach approaches the team and begins to explain the basics of baseball. He shares how to hold the bat, the importance of keeping your eyes on the ball, what direction to run, and the importance of touching the bases.

Throughout the season, the coach continues revealing the rules and regulations of the game. He shares lessons on strategy, sportsmanship, and being a good teammate. After just one year of baseball practice and games, it is not often that coaches can determine if a boy will make it to the major leagues as a player. But the first season definitely becomes the foundation of what is to come. Without realizing it, those early years of coaching in Little League often shape how one will approach the game, his preferred strategy, and the type of teammate he desires. These thoughts and acquired skills are sometimes transferable even into other types of sports or areas of life.

Early Coaching – Life Lessons and Emotional Blueprint

Life works in a similar way. Childhood is your first practice field. It's where you learn the rules of life. You begin to establish emotional survival skills, the mechanics of trust, and the unspoken code of how to behave. As it has been taught in many psychology circles, all behavior is reinforced. From the beginning, you recognize what gets you praise, what brings punishment, and what gets ignored. You take note of who approves, who disapproves, and under what conditions. You store this information, and over time it shapes how you see the world and how you see yourself.

Early childhood experiences can be viewed as your first round of coaching. These experiences—and the individuals connected to these experiences—grant opportunities for you to learn the game of life much like your Little League competitions and coaches gave you insight into the sport that you would come to enjoy for years. They create the personal stories you carry into adulthood, shaping how you build confidence, face challenges, and form relationships. If you are a man striving to meet the standards of strength, leadership, and masculinity that society sometimes expect, this early coaching is especially important.

Unbeknownst to you, when you were a boy, you had already been trained by your surroundings, your family, and the unwritten rules of your community about men and the subsequent expectations. You learned what was expected of you before you even had the ability to question those expectations. For example, maybe you grew up knowing that if you took out the trash, helped put furniture together, or fixed things that were broken, your mother would be pleased with you. You probably noticed that she didn't expect you to help cook, do laundry, or decorate the house; those tasks weren't part of what made you feel useful or valued. Over time, you began to connect your value at home to the chores you believed men were supposed to do. You told yourself, "If I do these things, the house is peaceful and I am appreciated. If I do something outside of that, it may be cool but it is not necessary."

Then the rules shift. As you get older, your mother begins to expect more from you. She begins to require things that she never asked for before. Now she wants you to help more around the house in ways that weren't part of your original expectations. When you can't meet these new expectations, she begins to say things that make you feel like you're falling short or that what you already do isn't enough. You might even feel unappreciated, wondering why the things that used to make her happy don't seem to be enough anymore.

In that moment, you learn an unspoken lesson that what used to be "good enough" for you as a man no longer is. Now you need to figure out what to do to keep her satisfied. So you start guessing and doing extra things at random, hoping to please her and feel valued again as a man. Just like that little boy on the baseball field needed his coaches to explain the rulebook, the strategy, and so much more, in order for you to gain a full understanding, you now need to reflect and unpack early recollections or past experiences as a key part of gathering a better perspective.

Formative Lessons – Family, Memory, and Manhood

I remember being a little boy, maybe four or five, and looking up to my oldest brother like he was the strongest big brother in our neighborhood. He was taller, faster, stronger, and smarter than me. But more important than all those attributes was the fact that he made me feel safe. From as early as he can remember, it was clear that he had been assigned the role in the family of protecting his little brother. Mom and Dad always reminded him, "Look out for your little brother," and to his credit, he took that responsibility seriously.

One memory in particular stands out. It stands out because of the feeling it left behind. We were going through a tough time as a family. Food was limited, and the weight of not having was something I could feel, even as a child. My mother had made a sandwich, the last of what we had, and she split it between me and my brother. I devoured mine without hesitation but remained hungry. My brother watched me carefully and intently before asking, "You still hungry?" I nodded, hoping that he would share. Without hesitation, he handed me his half. I ate it without thinking about what it cost him. Minutes later, someone knocked on the door with groceries, and that night we had more than enough to eat. Even now, I do not remember every detail, but I remember how it felt. The impact of that moment etched something into my spirit. It was a mix of sacrificial love, leadership, and instinctual protection. In that moment, without saying much, my brother coached me in what it meant to care for someone else's wellbeing above your own.

That experience would plant a seed that later shaped my identity and purpose. A few years later, our family grew to include a younger brother and sister. I instinctively tried to play that same role of protector that I had been taught by my brother. To me, protection meant preparation and prevention. I started helping them with homework, keeping them out of trouble, and warning them about the mistakes I had already made. It became second nature to lead through preparation and prevention as a form of protection.

Identity in Motion – Unpacking Your Playbook

What I didn't recognize then was how this behavior began forming a pattern that would show up again and again in different environments. Beginning in church, as an older child who was not quite a teenager, I took pride in helping the younger kids in Sunday school. As a teenager in high school, I was strongly encouraged to model a righteous path, especially as the son of a respected church leader. In college, I found myself mentoring incoming freshmen and working with young people in afterschool programs. I wasn't just doing good deeds. I was living out the lesson I learned from that shared sandwich on the kitchen counter.

Not every early lesson you carry is positive. Some are wrapped in trauma, scarcity, or neglect. Even when you try to bury these memories, they linger. They can shape you in ways you may not realize. These stories of survival sometimes crowd out the parts of you that could help you thrive. In your memories, you might see your parents or siblings masking their emotions. Maybe you remember only getting praise when you toughed it out. Or you remember being ignored unless you excelled. All of these moments sent subtle messages, training you to be who you are now. One of those messages could be that your worth is tied to performance, that strength means being tough or hiding your pain, and that leadership means staying emotionally distant.

Over time, you probably carried these unspoken "rules" into your friendships, your relationships, fatherhood, and even your work life. They show up as the anger we hold to prove toughness, or the emotional walls we build to avoid looking weak. The quintessential man who must protect and provide those he loves. The guilt that shows up when you don't meet standards. The standard is excellence only. You are not just expected to do the job, but to master it in order to be recognized for it.

These plays (or messages) were not invented overnight. They were coached into you from the start. Sometimes by parents. Sometimes by peers. Sometimes by life itself. If you can acknowledge that your early childhood experiences shaped your overall game plan or playbook, then you have to accept that some of the plays you're still running don't serve you anymore. Your brain didn't just record what happened in those early recollections, it locked in how you felt in the moment. And that feeling is part of your narrative identity.

Think of narrative identity like the story you tell yourself about who you are, where you've been, and what you're capable of doing. Picture it like your own personal movie. Every scene, good or bad, shapes the story of how you see yourself and your end goal. For example, maybe as a kid you missed the winning kick in a big kickball game, and everyone laughed. That moment might still whisper to you today: Don't take big chances. Play it safe. Or maybe you stepped up, hit a home run when no one believed you could, and now you believe you can handle anything when the pressure is on.

These stories, whether we talk about them or not, shape our confidence, our fears, how we deal with people, and even how we handle stress. That's why understanding your narrative identity is so important for your mental health. If you want to grow and get the right support, you first have to know the stories that keep playing in your head, so you can decide which ones help you and which ones hold you back. Research shows we all build our sense of self by stitching together memories like a highlight reel. This reel reveals and explains your greatest wins and toughest losses.

But as the game evolves, even seasoned players have to relearn how to relate, how to manage emotions, and how to lead with both strength and vulnerability. This doesn't mean you have to throw away everything you were taught. Many early lessons, like my brother's quiet act of handing me a sandwich when he thought I needed it, are worth keeping. That one small moment sparked something in me that led me to be more protective, helpful, and mindful of others' needs. Over time, that small piece of coaching turned into a part of my identity that I didn't even see clearly until I was grown. You have moments like this, too. Every man does, even if he hasn't dug them up yet.

Reflection, Repetition, and Rewriting the Playbook

Challenge yourself to revisit your early years, which are considered your first coaching. The power of early coaching is that it influences you whether you know it or not. Just like your dreams can reveal hidden thoughts and feelings, your earliest memories can help you understand yourself in ways you might not expect. When you start to look back, don't just focus on the big things, like moving to a new city, losing someone you love, going through hard times, or dealing with abuse. Those moments matter, but it's just as important to pay attention to the smaller memories too.

Think about who cheered you on when you were little. Who told you to "man up" when you were hurt? Who called you "soft" if you cried when you lost? These small moments may seem unimportant, but they helped build the foundation you're standing on right now. Often, it's the simple, everyday memories that say the most about who you are and how you see the world. These ordinary moments can reveal how you feel about yourself and other people, and whether you move through life with caution, hope, trust, or fear. They show the hidden patterns that still guide your choices today even if you haven't thought about them for years.

These are the pieces of early coaching that created your emotional and behavioral "muscle memory." If you want to grow beyond it, you have to become intentional about which parts of that old playbook still help you win and which ones you need to unlearn. Rewiring that emotional playbook isn't easy. It takes honesty, reflection, and sometimes outside help. But the reward is real: a fuller, freer sense of who you are, one that isn't driven by outdated rules or limiting beliefs, but by an honest awareness of who you really are and who you're becoming.

All of these moments blend into something even larger. Male identity is shaped through a complicated playbook of what the world tells you to be, what you see in real life, and how you respond. As previously noted, even as a young boy, you were picking up signals about what it meant to "be a boy." Maybe you didn't know it at the time, but you were studying the "coaches" all around you, in your parents, older siblings, neighbors, teachers, pastors, and neighborhood OGs.

Each of them cast you in a role, like a coach deciding if you'd pitch, catch, or warm the bench. Maybe you learned that being a boy meant staying tough, never talking back, or always finding a way to win. Maybe you watched your father work himself to the bone but never open up about what he felt. Maybe you saw your brother mask his pain with jokes. Those early lessons about masculinity stayed with you and traveled with you into every area of your life.

When you look back at these memories, be honest: Are you remembering what actually happened, or what someone told you happened? There's a big difference between your raw memory, what you really felt in that moment, and the version that was edited and hand delivered to you for consumption. Just like stats on a scoreboard, the story can get skewed if you don't check the tape. You might say, "I always struck out as a kid." But did you? Or did you strike out once, and an uncle laughed at you, and that moment became bigger than it really was? Or maybe you won the game, but no one was there to see it, so it didn't feel real.

Research shows that our memories can get distorted when we replay them through other people's commentary. A fascinating study from the Child Narratives Lab found that Black participants recalled more early memories and remembered them as more important and personally lived than White participants did. Black men, in particular, tend to rate these memories as vivid, meaningful, and rehearsed. By focusing on the meaning we attach to them, we may be able to change not just individual behaviors (the plays) but our entire approach to life (the playbook) simply by reframing our perspective.

In other words, your stories carry weight. These memories aren't just casual stories–they're lessons, warnings, motivations, and reminders. They show how you learned to navigate the world. If you can trace your early memories back, you can spot the patterns. And once you see those patterns, you can decide what to do with them. Some parts of your playbook can still help you win today. Things like the drive to protect, provide, or stay resilient no matter what. But others might be holding you back, like masking pain with anger or measuring your worth by how much you can endure alone. Your early memories are full of clues about these plays you are currently running. The question is whether you'll keep repeating them or start rewriting them.

The real work is looking at what shaped you, deciding what stays, and having the courage to change what doesn't help you anymore. So, when you sit down to examine your past, focus on what you remember. Don't just repeat the stories you've heard from your family about you being "the shy one" or "the troublemaker." Pull up the real footage, not just the story that got passed around the family.

Your early memories are not just random clips. They're your playbook. They tell you what shaped you, where you've been strong, where you got injured, and where you still have room to grow. If you want to play this life game really well–as a father, partner, brother, leader–then you must know what's driving your behavior. The better you know your first innings, the stronger you'll play the rest of the game. As we move deeper into this book, we'll explore how these early patterns show up in adult life especially in how we love, lead, and live with purpose. But it starts here: with awareness. By revisiting your own childhood "coaches," you begin to trace the roots of your behaviors and beliefs. You can honor what served you and release what didn't.

PAUSE, REFLECT, AND RECLAIM

Your early experiences aren't just things that happened; they're lessons you internalized, often without realizing it. They became the building blocks of your beliefs, behaviors, and expectations. The invisible rules you picked up as a child may still be running in the background of your adult life. The good news? You're not stuck with them. Just like any great athlete revisits old plays to improve their game, you can revisit your past to reclaim your future.

Before you move on, take a few moments to examine what early coaching has taught you—and what it's time to unlearn.

Pause, Reflect, and Reclaim

Ask Yourself:

◊ What is your earliest memory in life?

◊ What did it make you feel?

◊ How did it influence you?

Locker Room Wisdom:

"Every all-star once had a rookie season.

Review the early games that built your legacy."

CHAPTER 3

WATCHING FILM

RECOGNIZING PATTERNS

Opening Play – Patterns from the Past

Just like athletes study game footage to understand their strengths and weaknesses, you can learn a lot by looking back at your own behaviors and the family dynamics you grew up with. This kind of self-review helps you recognize the patterns that shape how you react when life puts you under pressure. Many of the ways you think, act, and handle stress today come directly from lessons you absorbed at home, at school, or from the people who influenced you when you were young.

These patterns are everywhere. They are entangled in your family's habits, the rules spoken and unspoken in your household, and the examples set by the people who raised you. Many Black families emphasize verbally or in action the value of hard work. This is evident in them holding multiple jobs or talking about side hustles. While this mindset promotes resilience and helps families survive and push through systemic barriers, it can sometimes overlook the other side of the equation, in ownership and business acumen. In a capitalist society, real power often comes from owning and building something of your own, so it's important to teach not just how to work within the system, but how to rise above it as an owner, an investor, or a leader.

These patterns are not limited to your home. They also show up in the second place where you spend most of your time as a child, which is school. As mentioned before, from the moment you set foot in school as a toddler, all the way through childhood, puberty, and your teenage years, you're shaped by constant feedback, judgments, and labels from teachers, administrators, and your peers. How others perceive you and how you begin to see yourself through their eyes also creates patterns.

These early experiences often plant seeds of either inferiority or superiority. Maybe you were praised for being smart, athletic, or well-behaved. Or maybe you were labeled as lazy, disruptive, or someone who was not living up to your potential. Over time, these messages become part of the story you tell yourself about who you are and what you are capable of.

As we have already discussed, you are constantly shaping your view of the world through these experiences. They build on each other and form the memories and early recollections that shape your narrative identity. At the same time, you begin to establish what you believe you can achieve.

In this chapter, we will look more closely at how to notice these patterns, where they begin, and how they show up in your daily choices. By understanding the roots of these patterns, you can begin to sort out which parts truly belong to you and which ones you are ready to let go of.

Breaking Down the Tape – Family, Triggers, and Mindsets

A personal example from my family is a pattern I have recognized in my own life, which is the drive to reach for something greater than what is right in front of me. My maternal grandfather really set the tone for this generational mindset. He began working at a very young age, stepping into adult responsibilities long before most children should have to. Even back then, he understood that life shouldn't be limited to clocking in and out, living paycheck to paycheck, and handing over your time in exchange for just enough to get by.

Through conversations with others and through his own observations, he realized that ownership was one way to break free from that cycle.

For him, he felt that land and business ownership could provide a path to something more lasting than an hourly wage. So, he worked hard, saved what little he could, bought property, and started a small business. Although this didn't lead to the kind of financial wealth he may have dreamed of and he still worked an additional hourly job until he retired, his willingness to believe in something bigger connected him to something different than wealth. He developed a spirit of progression, possibility, and determination that pushed him beyond limits that were placed on him during his time while tinder kindling for the next generation.

My mother took some sparks and turned them into a strong, steady flame. Growing up, I watched her navigate challenges that would have stopped many people in their tracks. She had a speech impediment that led people to underestimate her. Due to a lack of resources in her town, she lived with an undiagnosed learning disability that made her early education difficult. Yet despite these obstacles, she chose not to accept the low expectations others had placed on her. She went back to school, earned three advanced degrees, and built a career that reached far beyond the boundaries that her own upbringing suggested were possible.

Her example then showed me what was possible and what it looks like to keep moving forward even when the odds are not in your favor. Even though by most accounts I had a good childhood, I still felt a deep pull to build something bigger than what was shown to me. I knew early on that simply following the path laid out for me would never fulfill me in my life. So, I carved out my own lane, choosing to become a business owner and stepping into a career as a licensed therapist, a profession that's not always associated with Black men. I decided to claim space where I didn't always see people who looked like me.

When I step back and look at these three generations—my grandfather's willingness to try something new, my mother's determination to defy expectations, and my own journey of building and redefining success—I see a clear pattern. It's a pattern of entrepreneurship, education, resilience, and a relentless push to break past the limits of the previous generation. This shows me that what we inherit from our families isn't always money or land. Sometimes the most valuable inheritance is a mindset and belief in yourself.

Legacy Habits – When Survival Becomes Default

You cannot change what you do not first take time to observe. Patterns hold their own playbook of your life, so you need to watch the film closely. When you uncover the patterns in your life, you begin to see the deeper motivations and beliefs that guide your behavior. This is how you identify your triggers and develop healthier ways to cope and reach your goals.

In our current society, people often talk about being triggered without really studying their own patterns. You might think you are triggered by your boss criticizing you, but you may just dislike hearing what you are doing wrong. To truly know if something is a trigger, you must look back at how events, unspoken messages, and feedback shaped you from childhood up to now. For example, if your mother often called you out in front of your cousins and aunties at family gatherings and this was followed by teasing and laughter, then public criticism may truly be a trigger for you today. Understanding this gives you more control over your reactions.

Recognizing your triggers through honest reflection helps you avoid falling into the same habits that keep you from moving forward. One of the most effective ways to do this is by journaling. When you regularly write about your thoughts and feelings, you give yourself a record that reveals your emotional patterns. Over time, you will begin to see which situations consistently bring out certain reactions. This awareness allows you to connect the dots between past events and present emotions. By paying attention to these patterns, you position yourself to make intentional choices that move you toward growth instead of repeating the same missteps.

Lasting change only happens when you slow down enough to truly see what is happening in your life. Paying attention to your patterns does not require you to dissect every single moment, but it does call for moving through your days with more intention and honesty. This is more than just writing down what you did from morning to night. It is about pausing to ask yourself what you felt in certain moments, what fears might have influenced your actions, and what truths you wanted to speak but chose to hold back.

You could set aside a few minutes each evening to sit quietly and write about one or two moments that stayed with you. Maybe you felt embarrassed when someone corrected you in a meeting. Maybe you felt anger rise up when your partner asked you a question you did not want to answer. Do not judge these moments. Just write them down. Be specific. The more honest you are with yourself, the clearer the pattern will become over time.

When you look back through your pages weeks later, you will see which situations keep pushing the same emotional buttons. You might find that you always feel defensive when someone offers you help. Or you might notice that praise makes you feel suspicious instead of encouraged. These are clues that a deeper story runs beneath the surface.

Another important practice is to trace your feelings back to where they may have begun. Nothing in our lives happens in isolation. The way you react today is deeply connected to the way you learned to survive and adapt when you were younger. When you feel that tight knot in your stomach, ask yourself when you first remember feeling that same knot. Who were you with? What was said to you? What did you do to protect yourself back then?

For example, if you notice that you always feel angry when your work is questioned, think back to when you were younger. Maybe you had a teacher who embarrassed you in front of the class whenever you made a mistake. Maybe you had a parent who called you out in front of siblings and laughed about your failures. Those memories do not just disappear because you grow older. They hide in the background and influence how you respond when life makes you feel the same way again.

This is why self-reflection is so important. You can do this alone through journaling but talking with someone you trust can help too. Sometimes we need another person to gently point out what we cannot see for ourselves. A counselor, mentor, or close friend can help you see the bigger picture. They can remind you that you are not that child anymore and that you have the power now to respond differently.

Once you begin to see your patterns more clearly and understand what triggers you, you can practice responding in ways that build new habits and healthier outcomes. This is the work that turns self-awareness and emotional intelligence into real change. Start with small steps. When you notice a familiar trigger, pause before you react. Take a breath and remind yourself that you do not have to respond the same way you always have.

If public criticism is a trigger for you, and you know feedback in front of others makes you feel attacked, think about what you can do differently. You might calmly ask to have certain conversations in private. You might choose to listen fully before you speak. You might remind yourself that one person's opinion does not define your worth.

It can also help to practice simple grounding techniques when you feel your emotions starting to take over. One effective way is to use your five senses to bring yourself back to the present moment. Look around and name five things you can see. Notice four things you can touch. Listen to three things you can hear. Pay attention to two things you can smell. Find one thing you can taste. Using your senses like this helps you shift your focus away from the stress or embarrassment you feel and keeps your emotions from taking control of how you respond.

These small actions can interrupt long enough for you to choose a better one. Over time, these moments build new pathways in your mind. You are teaching yourself that you have options, that you are not powerless to your past, and that growth is possible when you stay present. Acknowledge your small victories as you grow. Pay attention when you face a familiar challenge and respond with more patience, self-control, or confidence than you did before. Even if you are not chasing trophies or medals, these moments are proof that you are building the kind of strength and discipline that leads to a fulfilling and successful life.

Rewriting the Playbook – Living with Intention

One of the most important truths you can hold onto as you grow is this: we repeat what is familiar because it is what we know, not necessarily because it is what is best for us. Many of the ways you think, speak, and act today began long before you knew what you were doing. These are your legacy habits. They are passed down through stories, family expectations, community norms, and everyday survival lessons.

Legacy habits are often enacted unconsciously. As children, we often learn habits such as the best ways to get attention from Mom or Dad. Maybe you learned to be loud and funny to be noticed, or maybe you learned to stay quiet to avoid conflict. Maybe you learned to please others to feel safe or to fight back to be heard. These strategies become second nature and follow you into adulthood, showing up in your relationships, your work, and your sense of self-worth.

The challenge is that while legacy habits can help us survive, they do not always help us thrive. They were created for the circumstances of the past, not the possibilities of your future. If you never pause to examine them, you might keep repeating the same cycles your parents and grandparents did without even realizing it. For example, you might believe working hard without rest is the only way to prove your value, or you might accept being the quiet one in the room because speaking up once caused you pain.

These old patterns shape how you respond to stress, handle criticism, or chase success. The problem is not that these habits exist, but that they often run your life without your permission. That is where awareness becomes your power.

While legacy habits run on autopilot, intentional behavior arises from conscious reflection and a deliberate choice to align your actions with the goals you have chosen for yourself. It means stepping back to ask, "Is this reaction helping me grow or just keeping me stuck?" It means noticing when you want to shut down, lash out, or give up, and then choosing a different path.

Living with intention does not mean you will always get it right. It means you trust yourself enough to catch the old habit, pause, and decide if that old way still serves you. This is how you break patterns that no longer fit the life you want to build. Instead of just doing what you have always done, you learn to act from a place of purpose and vision.

As you step forward, remember that your past is not there to shame you, but to teach you. Your family's struggles, your childhood lessons, and even your early mistakes all hold wisdom for you if you are willing to study them. Game changers study tape. Growth requires review. Locker room wisdom reminds us that champions, whether on the field or in life, win because they know how to study their past games and change how they play the next time.

PAUSE, REFLECT, AND RECLAIM

You cannot change the film of your past, but you can study it, learn from it, and write a new playbook for your future. So review your mental film reel for the patterns that hold you back and decide what plays need to change.

Ask Yourself:

◊   What behaviors or habits keep showing up in your life?

◊   When have you stayed true to yourself despite familial expectation? How can you continue to do this across the board?

◊   Think back to the type of person you wanted to be five years ago. What attributes did you have then that you don't think you have now? Is it preventing you from being your best self?

Locker Room Wisdom:
"Champions win not just by playing harder
but by studying the game they've already played."

Final Word: In the next chapter, we will go deeper into what really drives you and how to make conscious choices that match the future you want to create. It is not enough to just notice the old habits; you must understand what motivates you underneath them. What do you truly want? What values matter most? What choices will you make on purpose, not just by default? This is the work that turns awareness into action and old wounds into new wisdom. As you move forward, keep watching the tape. Keep asking questions. Keep choosing what stays and what goes. You are the author of your next chapter. Write it with your eyes open and your heart ready to let go of what no longer serves you.

CHAPTER 4

WHAT DRIVES YOU

MAKING CONSCIOUS CHOICES

Remember hearing the question "What do you want to be when you grow up?" Oftentimes you spit out the familiar jargon you heard from your peers or things you saw on TV or social media. Maybe you said you wanted to be a teacher, a firefighter, or a doctor. But more often than not, you probably said you wanted to be an NBA or NFL player. Rarely did you pause to ask yourself: What do I really value?

As we've said throughout this book, self-reflection and introspection are key in so many ways and that includes identifying your values. When you take time to honestly examine your past experiences, you'll start to notice where you felt most fulfilled, the activities you enjoyed, the goals you reached, and the moments you felt truly proud of yourself. You can also look at your roots to see that your beliefs and principles often come from that first coaching which shaped how you see the world, as we mentioned in chapter 2. These beliefs, combined with how you naturally react to different situations, form the core of your personal values. Knowing your values gives you guidance and direction. Think of your values like the bread-and-butter plays every great player keeps tucked in their playbook. When things get chaotic and they need something to keep them on course, those trusted plays guide them through.

As a child and sometimes even now as an adult, you are often told to dream big. But chances are no one ever taught you how to connect those dreams to your values. When people kept asking you, "What do you want to be when you grow up?" you probably did not realize your answers were planting seeds in your mind that shaped how you see success, purpose, and what is worth chasing.

Think about all the content you take in every single day. This constant flow of images, videos, and messages is an entertainment diet. A diet that can influence what goals you decide to pursue. Sometimes you follow those goals all the way through and reach them, only to feel emptier than ever. You hit the mark, but it doesn't feel right because you never took the time to ask where your real value lies.

When you slow down and pay attention to what certain experiences really mean to you, you start to see your true values more clearly. You also notice the emotional bonds and beliefs that bring you a sense of fulfillment. This awareness brings you closer to your core values. When you understand what truly matters to you, you do not feel worthless when you fail or when people disappoint you. Instead, you see those moments for what they are. They are lessons that help you grow. You can learn and keep going without losing your sense of worth.

You create success when your daily decisions match the man you say you want to be. To do this, you have to ask yourself better questions and be real with your answers. Who are you pursuing your goals for? What are you doing? When do you do it? Where do you do it? Why does it matter to you?

Who Are You Doing It For?

Be honest: how much of what you do right now is really for you? Think about your goals. Think about the job you grind at every day. Think about the side hustle you squeeze in at night. Think about the car you want, the clothes you wear, and the trips you post about online. Who are you really doing it for? Are you doing it to impress people you do not even talk to? Are you doing it to make your parents proud? Or are you doing it because this is what your heart wants and what your soul truly needs?

This is where you must understand the difference between intrinsic motivation and extrinsic motivation. Extrinsic motivation comes from outside rewards. It is doing things for recognition and rewards. Sometimes those outside rewards push you to train harder or stay focused when you feel tired. But if all you have is extrinsic motivation, you can still feel empty and unfulfilled after the applause fades away.

Intrinsic motivation comes from inside you. It is driven by your own love for what you are doing. Intrinsic motivation is what keeps you going when no one is watching. You train because it feels good and right in your spirit.

When you know the difference, you can make sure you are not moving just for the likes. You learn to feed your inner drive and build a life that makes sense to you even when the stands are empty. When you're clear about who you're doing it for, you stop living to prove something to everybody else. You start moving with intention. You protect your time, your focus, and your money because you know exactly where it needs to go, which is back into you and the life you're building.

What Are You Doing?

Next up: What are you actually doing? It sounds simple, but too many men are busy without being productive. You hustle. You stay "on the grind." But is that grind moving you forward or just wearing you out?

Back in 1990, Barbara Bush spoke to the graduating class at Wellesley College in Massachusetts. During her speech, she reminded the students how valuable family is and encouraged them to treasure their relationships with others with this statement: "At the end of your life, you will never regret not having passed one more test, winning one more verdict, or not closing one more deal," she said. "You will regret time not spent with a husband, a child, a friend, or a parent."

When you spend all your time working at a job or chasing a goal, you can end up neglecting the very things that make life meaningful and enjoyable. To avoid getting stuck in a cycle of just working for the prize, you need to get clear about where your time and energy are really going.

Write it down. Take out a sheet of paper and make a list of what you are actually working on each day. Look at your daily habits and remember that your habits shape your whole lifestyle. Ask yourself what is taking up most of your time. Think about what you say yes to and whether it matches what you truly want. Break it down in detail. Write what you are producing, what you are creating, what you are learning, and how you are improving.

When you write everything out, you can clearly see what matches your values and what does not. You can check how you feel about finishing certain tasks and projects. Sometimes you may catch yourself thinking, "What is even the point of this?" That thought is a signal that something probably does not fit who you really are or what you truly want.

You start to see what is building you up and what is draining your energy. Maybe you are pouring your time into things that have nothing to do with your real goals. Maybe you keep saying yes to distractions because you are focusing on the rewards or the applause and avoiding the more meaningful work.

Let me share an example from my own life to show what this can look like.

Some years back, before I opened my own small office uptown, I worked an entry-level job for a large Fortune 500 company. I took that job because I wanted some extra income to cover more expenses as my family grew. I started to do well at that company because I could learn, apply, and adapt to the methods they taught every employee. Before long, I was offered a chance to step into a small leadership role as a shift supervisor.

As I learned this new position, I saw how well the company paid its full-time employees and the good benefits they received. At the same time, I had always dreamed of running my own business. I had already started that journey before I took this part-time job. While I was paying the bills working for myself and working part-time at this big company, I started to think that if I stayed on their path and went full-time, I could reach the financial stability I wanted for my home.

I struggled with the choice. I had always pictured myself as my own boss. I wanted to create jobs in my community. I wanted the freedom to clock out when I needed to, not just for vacations but also to spend real time with my family. I wanted to be there for my kids' games, recitals, and events. Still, the money the company offered looked too good to walk away from, so I decided to chase the full-time position. In the end, I did not get the full-time spot. At first, I felt shocked and disappointed. But soon after, I felt a sense of peace. I realized that job did not line up with my true values.

I have always valued my independence and flexibility. I want to be present for my family and see my kids grow and achieve their goals. When that door closed, I had more time and energy to put into my own business. I found enough success to leave the company for good and still provide for my family, even though my income was less than what I might have made at the big company. But the trade-off gave me control over my own time.

During that period, my son discovered a sport that he loved and wanted to take seriously. Because I had control over my schedule, I could get him to practices and training sessions. I could show up for him fully. He finished his senior year in high school and hit every goal he set for himself in that sport. He told me how much it meant to him that I was not just cheering him on but was also there to help him get to matches, tournaments, and practices. It helped him earn the chance to compete at the college level.

Looking back, not getting that full-time position at the company turned out to be a blessing. It forced me to focus on what truly mattered and what fit my direction. Once I got clear on what I was really doing and why, I could cut away what did not serve me. I could put my energy into what lined up with the man I wanted to become and the father I wanted to be.

When Do You Do It?

Timing is everything. It is not just about what you do but also when you do it. It also matters how long you stick with it. Many men have big dreams but live as if they have all the time in the world.

For example, if you want to become a respiratory therapist, it is not ideal to wait until you are forty years old to go back to school. The program might only take two years, but age can make learning harder. As you get older, parts of the brain that handle learning and memory can shrink. Communication between brain cells can slow down. You may notice it takes longer to process and remember new information. This does not mean you cannot finish the program, but it does mean it could be more challenging than if you started sooner.

If your goal is to go back to school, make sure you set aside time to research schools and figure out how you will pay for it. Do not just say you want to go back. Sit down and write out a real plan. Include details like whether you will work and study at the same time or focus only on school. Write down your intended start date and when you expect to finish. Look into what kinds of jobs you want once you complete your degree or program. When you have a clear plan on paper, it becomes more real and you are more likely to stick with it.

If your goal is to build stronger connections, you must be intentional about how you spend your time. Block out time to truly be present with your kids, your partner, or the people you care about. Do not treat them like an afterthought you squeeze in when every other task is done. Make them a real priority on your calendar. Even if you are busy, you can choose to shut out distractions for an hour or two. Put your phone away. Turn off the TV. Give the people you love your full attention. These moments build trust, memories, and deeper bonds that last a lifetime.

If your goal is financial growth, set aside dedicated hours for learning new skills, planning your next steps, or building your side business. Make this time non-negotiable. You cannot just wish for more money or wait for someone to give it to you. You have to build a plan and put in the work day by day.

Maybe that means taking a course. Maybe that means meeting with a mentor. Maybe that means spending evenings working on your own project instead of scrolling on your phone. When you get clear on when you will do the things that matter, you set yourself up for real progress. Think of it like a game of football. There are moments during the game in which a play to keep the drive going is critical. Each player must carry out their specific assignment at the right time in order for the play to be successful and the drive to continue. The work that matters most needs timing, not just good intentions.

Furthermore, consistency does not happen by accident. It is built through small choices you repeat every single day. A few focused hours every week can change your life if you stick with it.

If you struggle with consistency, remember that planning your time gives you control. It keeps you from drifting from one task to the next with no purpose. It reminds you that your goals deserve space on your calendar just like work meetings or errands do. You cannot make progress if you do not make time. Be honest with yourself about what really matters and then protect that time like your future depends on it—because it does.

Where Do You Do It?

Your environment can either lift you up or hold you back. You are not just a product of your inner thoughts but also of the surroundings you choose and how you interact with them. People are always striving toward goals, but those goals are heavily influenced by the communities and spaces they move through. Where you choose to work, where you spend your free time, and where you connect with others all shape who you become and how far you can go.

Maybe you have dreams of writing a book, but you spend most of your time in places too loud to promote clear thinking. Maybe that same environment does not encourage you to read books that would help you learn how to write your own. Maybe you are not surrounded by people who would even help you share or promote your book when it is done.

Maybe you say you want to be more present in your relationship, but you spend all your free time at the driving range or at happy hour. You tell yourself it is networking, but the people you are with may not add any real value to your life or your goals.

Maybe you want to grow spiritually, but you never choose to be around people who share that same goal. You do not put yourself in spaces like a church, a small group, or a community where that kind of growth is possible.

If you stay in places that do not match what you want, your surroundings will hold you back instead of lifting you higher. Where you spend your time shapes what you build and who you become. If you want real change, you must choose environments that feed your mind, your spirit, and your purpose. In sports, home-court advantage matters for a reason. It's not just about the court, it's about energy and familiarity. Your surroundings can either cheer you on or weigh you down. Choose your field wisely.

Be willing to go where the growth can happen and be ready to leave places that keep you stuck. W. E. B. Du Bois once said, "The most important thing to remember is this: to be ready at any moment to give up what you are for what you might become." Let that be a reminder: changing your environment is sometimes the first step to changing yourself.

Ask yourself: Where am I spending my time? Is this place feeding my goals or starving them?

Sometimes the biggest change you can make isn't what you do, but where you do it. Find spaces that align with your values. Put yourself in rooms where people are working on similar things. Build an environment that makes your habits easier to maintain.

Your surroundings shape you more than you realize. Protect them.

Why Even Do It?

Here is the real fuel: your why. This is what keeps you steady when the grind gets hard, when you feel like giving up, and when distractions pull at you from every side.

If you do not know your why, you will end up chasing awards, seeking praise, and getting preoccupied with what other people say. You will spend your energy running after things that might not even matter to you in the end.

But when you know why you are doing something, you can stay focused and actually enjoy the ride instead of only looking at the finish line. You find joy in the process and not just the reward. You can practice what is called deferred gratification, which means you are willing to give up something small and tempting right now for a bigger and better payoff later.

When you have a clear why, you can say no to quick wins and easy distractions without feeling guilty. You know exactly what you are protecting with that no because you know what you are really saying yes to instead. You are saying yes to your bigger purpose. You are saying yes to the person you want to become.

Your why helps you keep your eyes on the bigger picture when it would be easier to settle for shortcuts. It gives you the patience to build something real and lasting. It makes the sacrifices feel worthwhile because you know they are leading you somewhere that matters. Hold on to your why and remind yourself of it every day. It will help you stand strong when the world tries to pull you in every other direction.

More than that, your why is your anchor. It is not just about money or status, although those things may come as part of the journey. Your why goes deeper than material rewards. It is rooted in what you value most. Maybe your why is to create generational wealth so that your children and their children never have to start from scratch the way you did. Maybe your why is to break the cycles you saw growing up, whether that means ending poverty, changing family habits, or building healthier relationships. Maybe your why is to feel free, healthy, and whole every single day so you can show up fully for yourself and for the people you love. Whatever it is, your why makes all the work worth it. It reminds you who you are and who you are becoming. It turns every sacrifice into a stepping stone instead of a stumbling block. It gives meaning to the late nights, early mornings, and hard choices.

When you know your why, you do not fold when challenges come. Instead, you stand firm because you know the bigger reason behind your actions. Never lose sight of your why. Keep it written down where you can see it. Talk about it with people you trust. Use it to check yourself when you feel distracted or tired. Your why is the fuel that keeps you moving forward when motivation runs out.

Every Decision Builds Momentum

You don't need a perfect plan to get started. You just need to start and then keep choosing actions that build on each other. Every decision you make is a chance to build momentum. When you lock in your Who, What, When, Where, and Why, you create direction. You don't wander. You build habits that stick because they make sense. They fit your vision. They match your values.

As you gather greater self-awareness and move with intention, you'll start to see a new truth: you must surround yourself with people who want to grow like you do. You need the right team. The right conversations. The right support. That's how you keep building momentum. In the next chapter, we'll dig into what it looks like to align yourself with like-minded people who can help you stay on track, push you forward, and remind you who you are when you forget.

PAUSE, REFLECT, AND RECLAIM

You've just walked through the core questions that shape your life's direction: Who, What, When, Where, and Why. These aren't just prompts for planning; they are a compass for finding your core values. Your choices should align with those values so they become steps to your ideal reality. Before moving any further, pause and reflect:

Ask Yourself:

◊ Who are you really doing this for?

◊ What activities or habits in your daily routine don't align with what you value?

◊ When do you prioritize what matters—and when do you avoid it?

◊ Where are you choosing to spend your time, and is that space helping or hindering your growth?

◊ Why does this goal, dream, or pursuit matter to you deep down?

Locker Room Wisdom:

"Your why is the heart and strategy of the playbook.
Without it, you're just running plays without purpose."

PART II
CONNECTION

We are not meant to move through life alone. Growth begins within, but it flourishes in connection. In this phase, you will step out of isolation and into deeper relationships with your brothers, partners, children, families, and communities. These chapters explore what it means to truly belong, to contribute in ways that matter, and to build emotional closeness that lasts. You will see how your early family roles and experiences have even shaped the way you connect and how healing can grow when connections are shared. This is where you learn to show up fully as a man others can trust.

CHAPTER 5

FREE AGENT PICKUP

SENSE OF BELONGING

The Dropped Baton – Why Connection Matters

True strength is in your capacity to connect. Developing and staying connected is a basic human need that helps you live longer, stay safer, and feel happier and stronger. Time and time again, research has shown that for humans and other animals, strong social ties are one of the best predictors of survival at every age. Having a variety of healthy relationships and social networks is key for your mental and physical health. That's why it's so important to look at how changes in the way you connect with others can affect things like mental health and physical illnesses. You may have learned to survive without connection, but you were always meant to belong.

In the game of life, you do not win alone. On a relay team, even the fastest runner depends on a good handoff. You may run your leg by yourself, and that can bring a sense of pride and power. But true victories come from smooth exchanges, when a trusted teammate is already in stride, ready to receive the baton, and the whole team moves as one. Somewhere along the way, maybe you picked up the message that you had to handle everything by yourself. Maybe you got good at carrying your own weight, staying silent when things hurt, acting like you didn't need anyone. Maybe you wore that like a badge of honor as the invincible loner, the iron man, or the one who never lets anyone get too close. But underneath all that strength, the same need lives in you that lives in every man: the need to truly belong.

The desire to belong is deeply rooted and shapes how you connect with others and find your place in the greater scheme of life. You can't outwork it, fake it, or bury it under achievements. It shows up whether you admit it or not. You feel it when you crave loyalty, when you want someone to stand by you, and when you hope your circle has your back. You feel it when you catch yourself trying to prove something or measure up to those early lessons you were taught. You remember what got you praise, what got you punished, and what got ignored. You learned all of that from the people you were connected to and the ones whose opinions mattered to you or whose approval you wanted. You feel it when you succeed and still have a sense of emptiness because no one's there to witness it with you. You don't have to keep pretending you don't need people. Connection is not a weakness, it is your lifeline. Without it, you are playing alone with no one to pass the ball to when help is needed. Connection is your insurance policy against isolation and despair. Men were never meant to be lone wolves forever. Even the strongest, most capable man needs a place to call home—and not just a physical home, but an emotional one.

True Belonging Is Not Just Being Seen, But Being Accepted

Think about the difference between being looked at and truly being seen. One scratches the surface but the other goes deeper and pulls out what is real. When you really belong, you do not just show the highlight reel like we often do on social media. You feel safe enough to share your scars, your flaws, and all your quirks. You do not feel the need to hide those parts or pretend they do not exist. Real belonging accepts you as you are, not just the version you think people want to see. When you belong, you don't have to perform. You stop acting for the crowd, stop putting on the mask just to stay included. You get to show up honestly. This does not mean you will never feel pressure or doubt yourself. It means you do not have to keep proving that you belong. Your people accept you as you are.

You have the freedom to be your true self and still stay connected to the group.

Wearing the jersey does not mean you are really in the game. True connection happens when you show up as your real self and trust your team to do the same. Is it possible that somewhere along the way, you have picked up the message that what you can do has more value than who you are? Your worth feels tied to how well you perform, not just to you being here. Growing up, you were praised for the points you scored or the grades you earned, but people rarely showed you how to handle or share your real feelings in the moment. The feelings of boys and men often go unnoticed and invalidated. Maybe you were told to toughen up, stop crying, do better, or be stronger. So you learned to measure your worth by what you could produce and not by the simple gift of your presence.

Without a sense of belonging, you overcompensate. Some men behave in such a way that it becomes toxic to their manhood, such as chasing multiple women, status, money, or trophies that make them feel important for a moment. Some men behave in a way that isolates them from the community by pulling away, hiding behind walls, avoiding risk. Either way, it comes from the same place. When you do not feel safe to belong as you are, you either try to prove you deserve it by becoming someone you are not, or you disappear and stop showing up altogether.

Cultural Expectations and the Mask of Disconnection

Cultural expectations can also make this harder. In recent years, the media has continued to box Black boys into narrow and often damaging stereotypes. Commercials, television shows, news stories, and other platforms regularly present Black boys as either the star athlete or the entertainer. They are also cast as the tough guy, the thug, or the gangster. On the opposite end of the spectrum, there is now a trend of depicting Black boys as overly feminine or as the poster child for gender fluidity and diverse expression. These repeated images imply that Black boys must fit into only these three identity lanes, each tied in some way to the idea that who they are is either entertaining, threatening, or confusing to the larger society.

Alongside the messages pushed by the media and society are the expectations we inherit from our own culture. These ideas have been handed down for generations through fathers, grandfathers, uncles, and the old heads in the neighborhood or barbershop. Their version of masculinity is known as traditional and rooted in the belief that a man should be strong, stoic, and able to handle everything on his own. But what happens when those same rules make it nearly impossible to admit you feel alone? What happens when you want to be open but your circle mocks you for showing any real Black boy joy?

You end up stuck, wanting real closeness but unsure how to ask for it without losing your place within the group. So you brush it off, crack jokes, pour another drink, or add another woman to your life instead of facing what you really feel. The need for connection does not disappear. It simply hides beneath the surface and quietly shapes your choices until those choices harden into your lifestyle.

Every team inherits plays from the past. But not every play still works in today's game. The culture may hand you outdated strategies—"be tough," "don't feel," "stand alone"—but at some point, you have to ask yourself if those plays are still winning you the game. I know this tension firsthand. Back in high school, I did not fit into any of those boxes. I was not an athlete or an entertainer. I was not the tough guy or the thug. And at that time, any idea of gender fluidity was out of the question for me. I was just a regular Black boy who liked sports but was never good enough to make the team. I loved to read and learn but had no special academic awards to brag about. I enjoyed church but always stayed in the background, avoiding any leadership role for people my age.

I dreamed of leaving my small town and making it big or simply going to college, even though my grades were way below average. I wanted to own my own business, get rich, and travel the country or maybe even the world. But those dreams felt too big to share with my circle at the time. So I mostly kept my thoughts to myself and stuck to agreeing with whatever my friends said about sports or girls.

Some people might say I simply did not find my community in high school. But I would argue that I did not find it because the cultural expectations were so clear to me back then. Where I grew up, you were supposed to be an athlete, stay out of serious trouble, get decent enough grades to land a good job, and then use that money to buy a nice car and live on your own in town. Anything outside of that script felt risky to say out loud. So again, I stayed quiet, played along, and kept my real hopes tucked away, preventing me from meeting more like-minded individuals that would actually influence me to reach for my dreams.

Choosing Your Relay Team – Building a Brotherhood

Contrary to what you may have learned growing up, you do not have to keep pretending to fit in with people who drain you or limit you. You have the freedom to choose who has access to your energy, your dreams, and your truth. You get to decide if you want to be surrounded by people who challenge you to stretch or people who keep you small because they have a limited view themselves. You get to decide if you want friends who clap for your progress even when you outgrow parts of who you used to be. You get to decide if you want relationships that hold space for your questions and your doubts without using them against you later. Choosing your team is just as important as choosing your goals. If the athletes don't reflect the kind of man you're becoming, it's time to make substitutions. Not everyone deserves a spot on the relay team.

Ask yourself what kind of brotherhood or friendship you wish to have. Maybe you need someone to simply say, "I see you, I hear you, and I have your back." Maybe you need a circle that calls out your bad habits but stays around long enough to help you build better ones. You can be that man for others while also attracting that same kind of loyalty. It is not about the number of people you know but the depth of trust you build with a few. That kind of trust does not grow overnight. It grows when you show your flaws, own your mistakes, and tell the truth about what you want from life. It grows when you prove that you will not run when things get uncomfortable.

If you look around and realize nobody knows you deeply, take that as a sign that it is time to move differently within yourself or maybe even outwardly through a new location. You do not need to broadcast your story to everyone. You need to share it with a few who have earned the right to hear it. You have to choose spaces where you do not have to shrink or edit yourself to belong.

Start by paying attention to the men you already respect but maybe never approached on a deeper level. Be the first to ask real questions. Be the first to listen without trying to compete. Be the first to say, "I want more for myself and I want to build with people who want the same." You will be surprised how many other men have been waiting for permission to say the same thing. When you show up open and willing, you set a new standard for brotherhood. You remind each other that you do not have to do this alone. Step by step, you can build a circle that sees you, checks you, and stays with you for the long haul.

After high school, I managed to get into college despite my less than stellar grades. From the very beginning, starting with summer orientation, I found my people. My first roommate was the most focused and disciplined student I have ever met, even to this day. He pushed me to develop real study habits and better ways to learn. I realized that cramming for an exam might help me pass, but it did not mean I truly understood anything. Real learning came from reading, talking about what I read, and applying what I learned every day. That first semester, I earned two As and two Bs, the best grades I had seen since eighth grade. I also met another friend who is still in my life today. He welcomed my entrepreneurial dreams and challenged me to think bigger about what I wanted for myself.

One day we were talking about how very few students of color were represented in student government. He looked at me and said, "So what are we going to do about it?" (Or something to that effect.) He pushed me to run for office and even made plans to run alongside me as our freshman year ended. By our sophomore year, we were both student senators. Even in sports, I got better because of the new friends I surrounded myself with. They would not let me slack off when we played pick-up games. They expected me to get better and they showed me how to level up. Each year, beyond pick-up games, I participated in several intramural sports.

By my senior year, I was part of a team that won the intramural basketball championship. Being in college opened my eyes to what it feels like to be around people who actually enjoy learning and want more for themselves than what they first saw at home or in their neighborhoods. We all came from different places, but each of us carried old expectations laid on us by coaches, teachers, church folks, and family. And for the parts of us that did not fit those expectations, we had each other to push for more. That push not only changed our own lives but also gave something better back to our families, our communities, and our people.

Reclaiming Your Place – From Isolation to Integration

Belonging is not about losing yourself to fit in with a crowd. It is about finding more of who you are alongside people who respect that version of you. True belonging means you know your presence makes a difference, your voice carries weight, and if you disappeared, you would be missed. When you reclaim your place, you stop lowering your standards just to stay in rooms.

Think about the men who raised you or influenced you along the way. Some of them taught you how to be strong but never taught you how to rest. Some taught you discipline but forgot to teach you connection. Some gave you loyalty but never showed you how to open your heart and receive love without suspicion. You do not have to discard what they gave you. You can honor the good parts while adding what was missing. You can become part of a generation of men who choose to hold both power and softness. You can be the man who knows how to protect but also how to be fully present. You can be the man who works hard but also knows when to let someone help carry the load.

None of this is about trying to get everything right every time. You should simply refuse to settle and decide to do better now that you know better. You should show up as a whole man and trust that you deserve to take up space in places where you do not have to cut off parts of yourself just to stay included.

So Where Do You Start?

Start with honesty. Look at the friendships and connections in your life right now. Who can you sit with and feel completely safe? Who leaves you exhausted every time you part ways? Who has challenged you to grow and who keeps you repeating the same cycles? Be real with yourself about what your circle brings to your life. If you want a connection that not only feeds you but sustains you, you cannot hold on to circles that provide calories but no protein.

Practice the art of being fully present when you're with people. Put your phone down, maintain eye contact, and really listen to what's being said rather than waiting for your turn to talk. When you show up engaged, you build trust and show respect. It doesn't matter if it's your coworkers, your boys, or someone you just met, the way you engage says a lot about what you value.

Finally, be proactive in seeking opportunities to meet new people. Step outside your usual circles and show up at networking events, community gatherings, or workshops that align with your interests. Join a running club, volunteer, or strike up a conversation at a school council meeting. Every new connection has the potential to challenge you, sharpen you, and expand your world.

The truth is, real connection doesn't just fall into your lap. You have to go after it, work at it, and guard it once you have it. The more effort you put in, the more fulfilling your life will feel. This is how you turn that quiet feeling of isolation into genuine brotherhood. This is how you choose real community instead of choosing fakeness. This is how you become intentional about developing friendships to experience life with others.

Free Agent No More

Maybe you have felt like a free agent for too long, moving from one group to another without ever feeling like you truly fit in or could trust that you had a place to land. It is time to put on the jersey and claim your place on the team. You belong here, not because you have it all together or because you always perform at your best, but because you are human and humans are built to need one another. Never forget that your real strength is in your willingness to connect. You can lift heavy, work hard, and run faster than most, but you cannot outrun the part of you that needs real connection. The good news is you do not have to keep running. You get to build real bonds little by little, truth by truth, and moment by moment when you show up as you are. Choosing connection is not weakness; it is wisdom. It means you know that no man is meant to carry every burden alone. Brotherhood, friendship, and community are not luxuries, but rather, they are necessities. When you own that truth, you give yourself permission to build relationships that remind you who you are and what you are capable of becoming when you do not stand alone.

Real belonging doesn't require performance; it requires presence, vulnerability, and intention. It requires you to stand in your own story and let others stand with you. It asks you to trade the mask for your real face, the lone wolf badge for the brotherhood you deserve.

Once you understand where you stand in terms of connection, the next step is learning how to contribute. Belonging is the foundation but contribution is how you strengthen it. When you know how to bring your best to the group, you help everyone grow stronger, including yourself. So take this moment to look inward. Ask yourself the hard questions. Decide what you want to keep, what you want to leave behind, and who you want to build with. You were never meant to do this alone. Pick up your jersey. Claim your spot. Belong.

PAUSE, REFLECT, AND RECLAIM

You weren't meant to play alone. You were meant to belong. But true belonging begins with you being honest about who you are and what kind of connection you desire. Before you move on to the next chapter, take a moment to reflect. These questions aren't just mental exercises—they're your chance to rewrite the plays that no longer serve you and draft a game plan that centers on belonging and authenticity.

Ask Yourself:

◊   Who are the people in your life you feel most yourself around?

◊   In what ways have you been performing instead of showing up honestly?

◊   What old expectations are you still trying to meet that no longer reflect who you are?

Locker Room Wisdom:
"You were never built to play this game alone.
There is strength in community, not only because of the support it
provides but also because of the differences it brings together. When
you combine different perspectives, you create room for sharper
strategies and better solutions."

CHAPTER 6

LEARNING YOUR POSITION

CONTRIBUTION

Each Position - Know Your Role on the Field

Think about any great football team. Every player, from the quarterback to the lineman to the kicker, has a specific role that supports the overall game plan. If the lineman tries to play quarterback, the whole team suffers. Success happens when each man knows his position and executes it with discipline. Life is no different. Knowing your position, where you serve best, where your strengths shine, and where your presence makes the biggest impact is the foundation of a purposeful contribution.

We are motivated by our need to contribute. We all want to know that we matter and that what we do means something. There was a psychologist named Alfred Adler who believed that deep down, people want to help others and give back to their community. He called this idea social interest. Basically, it means that looking out for your people and giving back is what makes life feel real and worth it. This shows up in how you work with others and how you care about what happens to them. According to Adler, nobody is born automatically knowing how to care about the bigger community. For a lot of men, that sense of responsibility has to be taught and encouraged through good parents, solid friendships, and those who lead by example daily. When you learn how to care about others and play your part, you find real meaning by helping make life better for everybody around you. Your worth doesn't just come from standing out in a crowd. It comes from showing up when it counts. You were never meant to play every position on the field. A good team works because each player knows his spot, understands his strengths, and steps up when it's time. Try to play every position by yourself and you'll wear yourself out and let your people down anyway. But when you know where you fit, you can put your energy where it matters, grow your skills, and be there when your people need you. Giving back and doing your part isn't about chasing praise. It's about building trust, feeling proud of who you are, and having a purpose that shows through your actions. That's how you move from just existing to actually making an impact that people can feel.

Striving for Superiority – Why We Reach to Contribute

Adler believed that all people struggle with feelings of not being good enough at some point in life. Psychologist Kenneth Clark took that idea further and showed how this plays out specifically for Black people in America. He pointed out that segregation was a powerful way for society to tell Black folks they were "less than." Generations of Black children were forced to attend underfunded schools that were clearly worse than the ones other children went to, and that sent a clear message about who was valued more. It did not stop at schools. Every part of society, from buses to restaurants to neighborhoods, was designed to remind Black people that they were seen as second class. Over time, this message wears down a person's sense of self-worth. Many of us still carry that old message which shows as a lie that we are not as worthy. The message gets passed down unless we confront it directly through therapy, open conversations, or any other tools that help us heal. If we do not challenge that feeling of being less than, it continues to live within us and our communities.

So what do you do with that feeling? You strive for superiority. You work hard to prove you matter. You look for ways to stand out, to shine, to prove to yourself and others that you're not just average. You earn degrees, chase job titles that set you apart, or buy name-brand things to show your status. This drive can help you grow, but it can also fool you into believing that you only matter when you are better than someone else. When that happens, you stop working with others and start competing against them. Competing often leads to constant comparison, and as the saying goes, "Comparison is the thief of joy." Comparison is a trap that steals your peace and your focus. The key isn't to stop growing but it's to shift your mindset from proving you're better than someone to asking how you can be useful to someone. That's the difference between chasing status and living with real social interest. One satisfies your ego. The other restores your soul.

When You Help, You Heal

Sometimes the most powerful move isn't taking the last shot, it's the assist for the win. When you choose to serve instead of seeking the spotlight, it shifts the whole energy of the team. That kind of selfless contribution not only uplifts others, it restores something in you. It reminds you that impact isn't always loud or flashy; sometimes it's quiet, intentional, and deeply healing. One of the quickest ways to break free from isolation, which can lead to loneliness and even depression or anxiety, is to help someone else. When you help others, you step out of your own head. You stop dwelling on past mistakes or obsessing over your wins and instead focus on being useful. When you show up for a friend or a neighbor, you do not prove your worth by talking about it but by demonstrating it through your actions. Taking action builds pride. Taking action creates purpose. You begin to see yourself as someone who makes a difference, no matter how big or small that difference may be.

I see this play out in my own life as a therapist. Helping other people manage their anxiety and grief has actually helped me handle my own. There are times when I walk clients through simple things like deep breathing, reminding themselves that just because they have a thought does not mean it is true, or grounding themselves by tuning in to their five senses. When they come back and tell me they tried it and it worked, it gives me proof that what I do matters. But it does even more than that when it reminds me that I need those same tools too. I teach them, but I also use them for my own battles.

Think back to a time when you helped someone who needed it. Maybe you helped a friend move, gave your brother some advice, or stayed late to help a coworker finish an important project. How did you feel afterward? You were probably tired, but you also likely felt good because your presence mattered. That is the power of contribution. You do not have to save the world, but you do need to be willing to serve the part of the world you can touch. The groups you are part of which are your family, your friends, your team at work—they all need you. Maybe they do not need you to be the hero, but they do need you to be reliable. They need you to show up and handle the small things that keep the bigger things working. Your contribution does not have to be big or flashy. Most of the time, it is the consistent, quiet actions that make the biggest impact: checking in, showing up on time, doing your part without complaining, and backing up your words with follow-through. Helping others humbles your ego in the best way. It reminds you that you are part of something larger and that your role truly matters.

Know Your Position – Play Your Position

When you try to play every role, you end up out of position. The win comes when each man owns his space and trusts the system to work as it should. One big reason a lot of men burn out is because they do not know how to stay in their lane. A lot of stress comes from trying to force yourself into a role you wish you had instead of working with the one you actually have. Maybe you learned early on that being needed made you feel valuable, so you said yes to everyone and everything. You carried too much and wore yourself out trying to keep everything together. This shows up at work too. You might be stuck in the background while someone else gets the promotion you know should be yours. Or maybe you try to be the wise veteran but people just see you as the old guy who has been around too long. Ultimately, you have a few options or roles that you can play, even if it feels like settling. You can tweak the role to fit you better, or you can push to change the whole setup to create something that works for you. One can have you feeling like giving in a little and the other can wear you down. Another option is to leave, which might feel like taking a loss or paying another cost.

Knowing which move to make takes real wisdom, but even then there is no perfect answer. There is always some kind of trade-off. What you do not want to do is keep pushing yourself into a role that does not match what is happening around you. That is like calling a play and executing when nobody else is executing. That is how you end up tired, frustrated, and out of place. Here is the truth. You are not built to carry every role by yourself. If you are trying to be the quarterback, the coach, the trainer, the water boy, and the general manager all at once, you are headed for burnout and resentment.

When you know your position, you save your energy for what you do best. You trust your team to handle what they need to handle. You focus your time and effort on the role that matches your strengths. You do not waste hours trying to be the hero in spaces you were never meant to lead. You also give other men room to step up and handle their business too. When you try to take on everything by yourself, you block other men from stepping into their roles and growing into their responsibilities. You end up tired and frustrated, and they stay uncomfortable on the sidelines as they wonder when they will get their opportunity. Real teamwork means everybody has a part to play and everybody does their share. Staying in your lane is not about being selfish or lazy. It is about protecting your energy, trusting your brothers, and playing your position so the whole squad wins. You have enough on your plate already. You do not have to prove your value by doing everyone else's job too. Show up, play your part well, and let the next man do his.

You Don't Have to Be the MVP – Just Be Clutch in Your Role

What counts most is showing up when it matters, bringing energy, consistency, and heart when others are running low. Every winning team relies on the quiet strength of those who deliver when the pressure is highest. One of the biggest lies many of us believe is that we only matter if we are the star of the show. But think about any team that has won a championship. They do not win because one guy does it all by himself. They win because everybody on that roster, from the bench player to the starter, shows up and does his part. Take a look at the game of basketball. The players seven through nine rarely, if ever, have their name in lights, but they are the ones who keep the game alive when the starters need a break. Their minutes matter. The bench keeps the energy steady when others are tired. They may not get the same headlines as the star players, but if you ask any team, they will tell you how much they depend on them to keep things moving when it matters most.

Life works the same way. You may not be the loudest one in the room. You might not run point or be the one giving the big speech. You might not be calling every shot. But if you know where you fit and you do what you do well, you are just as valuable as the star player. You are the one who keeps things steady when others cannot. Too many of us waste time trying to play someone else's position when our true value is right where we are. A real man does not compete with his teammates. He completes them. He makes everybody better by doing his part well. So stop thinking you have to be the face of everything to matter. Sometimes the most powerful impact you have is when you hold it down in the role you were built for. Know your position. Do it with pride. And trust that your contribution keeps the whole team winning.

Know Your Strengths and Show Up

In every sport, a winning team is built on complementary roles. The rebounder, the shooter, the defender, and the playmaker all matter. You win not by doing everything, but by doing your job with excellence. When a player knows his strengths and executes them consistently, the team becomes unstoppable. Again, picture yourself on a basketball court for a second. Every good team needs more than just a star scorer. Somebody has to run the offense, somebody has to grab the rebounds, somebody has to lock down on defense, and somebody has to speak up in the huddle when the game is on the line. So how do you figure out what your role is on your team, whether that is at work, at home, or in your community? It starts with knowing what you naturally bring to the game. Maybe you are the throwback point guard type, the one who can bring order when everybody else is scattered and the play has broken down. Maybe you are the steady voice, like the veteran on the bench who calms the younger guys and prevents them from getting out of control when pressured by the opponent's crowd. Maybe you are the hype man, the teammate who keeps the energy high when everybody's legs are getting heavy in the fourth quarter. Or maybe you are the quiet one who sees when something is off with a teammate and checks in behind the scenes to make sure he is good to go for the next play.

No role is too small to matter. The truth is, what makes you valuable is not trying to be like the next man but really understanding who you are and putting that into motion every single day. When you know your game, you can play it with confidence. You do not have to force shots that are not yours. This is where emotional intelligence shows up. It is like reading the floor in real time. You pay attention to what is happening inside you and around you, and you choose how to respond instead of just reacting. When you understand yourself better, you know how to contribute in a way that lifts the whole squad.

But just knowing what you do well is not enough. It does not mean anything if you do not bring it every time you step on the court. Consistency beats raw talent every single time. People trust a man who does what he says he will do. Trust is the glue that holds teams, families, friendships, and partnerships together. It is hard to get close to a man who only suits up when it is convenient for him. Real connection comes when people know they can count on you in overtime and in practice, not just when the lights are bright. If you say you will show up, show up. If you cannot, say so. Do not vanish when the game gets tight. Be willing to box out, dive for loose balls, and do the unglamorous work that keeps the team together. When you show up over and over again, people stop wondering if you are all talk. They feel safe putting their trust in you because they know you are not going to disappear when things get real. That trust is worth more than any highlight reel moment you could chase trying to do it all alone. Knowing your strengths and showing up every single time makes you the kind of man people want on their team every day of the week.

Purpose, Not Performance

Don't just play for the crowd or the praise, play for the love of the game. The scoreboard doesn't show the hustle plays, the screens set, or the quiet leadership in the locker room. But those are the very things that win games. Likewise, your purpose matters more than your applause. When you contribute from your real position, you build a sense of purpose instead of just chasing stats. You get to stand in the truth that you made life better for the people around you. Your value does not swing back and forth based on who shouts your name or how many times you get patted on the back. You stop looking at the next man's role wishing you had his shot because you finally see how every role works together to win the game. You understand that your steady effort behind the scenes keeps everything moving. You might not always get the highlight clip, but you get something deeper—real respect that is built on trust and on what you actually do when no one is watching.

Men who know their position grow stronger than men who try to do it all. They focus on sharpening their skills instead of wasting energy chasing every opportunity that pops up. They do not lose sleep comparing themselves to somebody else. They invest that time getting better at their own craft and showing up solid every single day. They know that greatness is not about doing everything but about doing their part well enough that other people can count on it. Knowing your lane also protects you from burning out. You do not have to carry every burden on your back. You do not have to lose sleep worrying about things that were never your responsibility in the first place. You can rest easy knowing you have done your part and done it well. And you trust the people around you to handle theirs too. When you play your position with intention, you free up your mind and your energy to stay ready for what is really yours to carry. That is when you find real pride. Not just in what you do but in who you are and how you lift up the people counting on you to show up ready every time.

The Power of Showing Up

Championship teams aren't built on talent alone, they're built on consistency. The player who shows up for every practice, gives effort in every drill, and keeps his word is the one the coach can trust. That kind of consistency off the court wins just as much as skill on the court. In life, being dependable is the true mark of greatness. When you understand your role and show up for other people, you begin to see that your value is not about being the best man in the room but about being dependable and useful. You become someone people can trust because you keep your word and handle your responsibilities without excuses. You earn real respect by delivering on what you promised instead of just talking about what you could do. Each time you come through for your people, you strengthen your bond with them and prove you can be counted on when it matters most.

When you contribute, you shift your focus from just thinking about yourself to thinking about the people around you. It pulls you out of your own head and places you right where you can make a difference that others can feel. It gives your days more direction because you know your energy is going somewhere that matters. You start to feel that your time and effort have a purpose that is bigger than just looking good for the moment.

Knowing your position brings you a sense of pride because you know exactly what you bring to the table. But real connection does not stop at just doing your part. It grows stronger when you decide to build real closeness with the people around you. Brotherhood, deep friendship, and intimacy all get stronger when trust turns into closeness. And that closeness is where the real magic happens. That is what we tackle next.

PAUSE, REFLECT, AND RECLAIM

Take a moment to step back from the hustle. Reflect on what you've just read and ask yourself what it really means for your journey.

Ask Yourself:

◊   Have you been trying to play every position instead of staying in your lane? What are the signs that it's time to reset and trust your teammates?

◊   Think about a time when your quiet contribution made a big impact. What did it teach you about the power of showing up?

◊   What's one way you can be more consistent this week—on and off the field?

Locker Room Wisdom:
"You don't win the game by doing it all.
You win it by doing your part and doing it well."

CHAPTER 7

LOCKER ROOM CAMARADERIE

BUILDING EMOTIONAL CLOSENESS

"Each of us has an innate need to feel safely attached to another person who will be there in our times of physical or emotional need." – Dr. Susan Johnson

You can tell the strength of a team by what happens after the final whistle. When the noise fades and the scoreboard lights go out, the real connection shows up, in the quiet support, the shoulder-to-shoulder silence, and the presence that needs no performance. That's where true camaraderie lives. Think about the tight bond of a locker room after a big win or even a tough loss. Teammates pat each other on the back, laugh together, vent frustrations, or just sit in silence. That sense of knowing someone has your back is exactly what Dr. Susan Johnson is talking about. Feeling connected means feeling close to people who genuinely care about you. Most people know kids need a safe bond with a parent, guardian, or trusted peers who look out for them. What we often forget is that adults need the same thing. You need it. I need it. Every man you know needs it. A secure, caring connection with another person helps us get through life's ups and downs.

Once you understand that people are built to develop and maintain strong connections, you start to see why your mind and heart are always looking for intimacy, emotional closeness, and signs of a solid relationship. When you feel that bond slipping through constant arguments, emotional distance, or awkward silence, it creates a deep unease. Just like a team can fall apart without trust and support of their coach or each other, your well-being depends on feeling safe and close to the people who matter most. That need does not end when you graduate, get a degree, secure a career, or build a family. In other words, the need for connection does not end in childhood. Adults need connections to feel whole.

Your Brain Is Wired for Connection

You have been designed for connection since day one. It is not an accident that you crave closeness or miss it when it is gone. Scientists have found over and over again that human brains are social brains. You gain energy and confidence through meaningful ties with others. You grow stronger when you feel supported and know you do not have to carry every burden alone. When you have people who truly see you, hear you, and stand with you, it affects how you move in the world. You hold your head just a little higher. You take more calculated risks because you trust you have support if you should fall. Studies show that men with healthy, emotionally secure relationships have lower stress levels, stronger immune systems, and longer life expectancy.

On the other side of connection is loneliness, and it serves as a real health risk. The Centers for Disease Control and Prevention report that loneliness and isolation can lead to serious mental and physical health challenges. They associate social disconnection with higher rates of heart disease, stroke, dementia, type 2 diabetes, depression, anxiety, and even early death. Interestingly, loneliness has become so common that it is now considered an epidemic even though we are more digitally connected than ever. There are men with hundreds of followers on social media and many others they can hang out with but no one they can really open up to. Men can post intimate information randomly on multiple platforms or DM a stranger in seconds but struggle to sit down and talk face-to-face about real feelings. Men seem to share in therapy that they keep their circle small but locked tight because the fear of vulnerability feels bigger than the fear of isolation.

Why Secure Bonds Matter at Every Age

If you have ever wondered why you struggle with closeness or why trust feels risky, you are not alone. Attachment theory, first introduced by John Bowlby and expanded by Mary Ainsworth, explains why some of us naturally feel safe opening up while others find it hard. Attachment theory says your earliest relationships shape your understanding of closeness.

If you had a caregiver who was dependable, kind, and attentive, you learned that the world is safe and people can be trusted. You developed a secure attachment style. You probably find it easier to connect with others now because your mind was wired to expect connection to feel good. If you had a caregiver who was unpredictable, harsh, distant, or absent, you might have learned to protect yourself by pulling back or clinging too tightly. These patterns do not disappear when you grow up. They follow you into friendships, family life, and romantic relationships. They show up in how you argue, how you apologize, how you forgive, and how you love.

The good news is you do not have to stay trapped in old patterns forever. You can learn to build secure bonds even if your start was not the best. By adding vulnerability, trust, shared experiences, and emotional availability, you can create and strengthen your connections. Every choice you make to lean into these qualities brings you closer to the kind of connection you truly deserve.

Vulnerability: The Secret Strategy

The strongest players don't just push through pain, they speak up, lean on their team, and ask for help when it counts. Vulnerability isn't weakness; it's the strategy that keeps the game real and the bonds unbreakable. One reason so many men keep an emotional distance is that it requires something many of us were taught to avoid: vulnerability. Vulnerability means being open enough to let someone see you as you really are. It means letting your guard down long enough for someone to step in and support you. It is risky. No doubt about it. But it is also the only way to build trust that goes deeper than surface talk. When you let someone see your fears, hopes, mistakes, and truths, you give them a chance to meet the real you. You also show them it is safe to bring their real self to the table. Vulnerability opens doors that would stay locked otherwise.

After I graduated from college, I worked at a few jobs where my relationships with coworkers and my supervisor stayed on the surface. We laughed and joked during work hours, but we never moved beyond casual conversations and small talk. Because of that, it was hard for me to ask for help, share concerns, or talk openly about my goals for the future.

Then I landed a job where my supervisor and my coworkers made it safe to be vulnerable. We would gather for lunch every day and hold meetings twice a month that encouraged us to open up. As we spent more time together, we found ourselves talking about things that really mattered to us. We shared stories about our families, our friendships, our interests, and the activities we enjoyed outside of work. That openness changed how I communicated. It made it easier for me to ask questions about where our department was headed. I learned new skills informally just by listening to my supervisor share her experiences and lessons from her career. Those lessons shaped me into one of the best in my position. My coworkers and I also leaned on each other and looked out for one another. We lived out the saying "each one, teach one" every day. The willingness to be vulnerable in that workplace created bonds that strengthened our work and made us better employees. Since then, I have not experienced that same level of vulnerability in any other job. That time showed me just how powerful vulnerability can be when people allow it to exist.

Some may look at vulnerability as weakness but they should see vulnerability as courage in action. It is the courage to say you do not have it all figured out. It is the strength to admit you need help. It is the boldness to forgive or ask for forgiveness. Brené Brown, a researcher who has spent years studying connection and courage, says that vulnerability is the birthplace of love, belonging, creativity, and joy. When you allow yourself to be vulnerable, you also give yourself permission to imagine new ideas and see possibilities that fear would block. You cannot build meaningful connections without it.

Trust Is Earned Over Time

In any high-stakes game, trust isn't given, it's earned through every small moment: the pass that gets made, the coverage that doesn't break, the follow-through on the play. Consistency builds confidence. That's how trust wins the long game. If vulnerability is the doorway, trust is the foundation. You do not build trust overnight. It is earned over time through repeated actions, honest words, and a willingness to show up even when it is uncomfortable. Trust means you believe another person will not harm you on purpose. It means you can count on them to handle your truth with care. We live in a world where trust is fragile because so many people have been hurt by those who promised not to hurt them. That is why your actions matter more than your talk.

Trust grows when you say what you mean and do what you say. Trust grows when you follow through. Trust grows when you choose compassion over judgment. Trust grows when you communicate clearly instead of letting silence or assumptions poison your connection. Trust is like a savings account. Every act of kindness, every moment of honesty, every show of reliability deposits something into that account. When conflict happens, that trust account keeps you from going bankrupt and losing a healthy relationship. Whether it is with your brothers, your partner, or your circle of friends, trust is the bedrock. Without it, nothing healthy stands.

Shared Experiences Make Bonds Stronger

Championships aren't built in a single game, they're forged in shared practices, long bus rides, early mornings, and hard-fought moments. It's not one play that builds trust, but the journey taken side by side. Think about your closest friends. Chances are you did not bond over a single moment. You bonded through a series of shared experiences. You might have been classmates, teammates, or roommates. You enjoyed the same activities, suffered through the same losses, worked late nights together, or tackled challenges side by side. Those shared moments create a kind of shorthand between people. You do not have to explain every detail because you lived it together. Shared experiences build inside jokes, quiet understanding, and deep loyalty.

With intimate relationships, couples who share interests and experience them together tend to have stronger, happier relationships for the same reason. Partners who enjoy similar adventures, hobbies, or goals invest their energy in the same direction. They fight less because they have fewer disagreements over how to spend time and money. They fight smarter because they see each other as teammates, not opponents. When you share life with others, you multiply joy and divide burdens. You celebrate together and grieve together. Whether it is pick-up games, book clubs, road trips, or Sunday dinners, shared experiences matter. They turn casual acquaintances into a chosen family.

Emotional Availability Is Contagious

The energy you bring to the huddle spreads fast. When one man speaks up with honesty, it invites others to drop their guard too. Openness multiplies. It's how real teams build chemistry, and real relationships build trust. Have you ever walked into a room where people were laughing so hard that you started laughing too, even though you had no idea what the joke was? Have you ever sat beside someone who was crying and found yourself tearing up with them? That is emotional contagion at work. Research on emotional contagion shows that we naturally pick up on the emotions of people around us. We do it because we want to connect. We do it to understand what others are going through. We do it to show we care. This is why you catch yourself matching a friend's excitement or feeling your partner's frustration even when their problem is not yours to solve.

Emotional availability spreads the same way. When you make it safe for people to bring their real emotions to you, you create space for honesty. You help them feel truly seen and understood. In return, they are more likely to hold that same space for you when you need it. It becomes a feedback loop that makes closeness grow stronger over time. This is part of what people mean when they talk about emotional intelligence. Emotional intelligence is not just a buzzword. It is your ability to recognize your own feelings and pick up on the feelings of others and then respond in a way that builds trust. You do not have to be a mind reader to do this well. You just need to pay attention and stay open. Emotional closeness does not happen just because you check off a list of good behaviors. It happens because you are willing to listen when it is uncomfortable, share when you would rather stay silent, and show real empathy even when you do not have all the answers. That is what makes connection last.

A Team That Has Your Back

Even after a tough loss, the best teams regroup not by blaming, but by leaning on each other. They remind one another: the season's not over, and neither is the story. Brotherhood is built in those moments. You may have learned how to build your success on your own because doing it alone was the only way you knew how to survive. Maybe you had to carry yourself through challenges without much help from anyone else. That kind of strength deserves respect. But at this point in your life, you need more than solo victories. You need a solid circle that will celebrate your wins and stand beside you when you take a loss. A real brotherhood does not waste energy trying to see who can hide the most and wear the best mask. A real brotherhood pushes each man to show up fully, especially when life is heavy. When you have that kind of connection, you do not feel the pressure to pretend.

My two brothers and I meet for breakfast every Saturday morning, no matter what. Even if one of us cannot make it, the other two still show up. What started as simple breakfast gatherings turned into real check-ins with each other. Over time, those meals opened the door for us to share our struggles, admit when life feels heavy, and become more aware of what we are really carrying day to day. Those Saturday mornings became our safe space to talk about the hard things we face as men. They turned into moments of honesty and moments of brotherhood. We talk about our roles as husbands, our responsibilities as fathers, and the ways we try to lead our families well. Week after week, we remind each other that we are not alone in this work. What began as a meal has grown into deep conversations that keep us grounded. We leave those breakfasts feeling stronger, knowing our brothers will have our back, and even more clear about what really matters. That time together reminds us that showing up for each other is one of the best ways to keep showing up for our families.

Think back to the feeling in a locker room after a tough loss. Everybody knows the scoreboard says they fell short. But they lean on each other anyway. They talk it out, they lift each other's heads, and they remind each other that the story is not over. Then they walk out of the building together, already thinking about what needs to happen to come back stronger next time.

What It Takes to Build This Kind of Bond

You build this kind of closeness by considering your presence and your honesty. You build it by showing up for people even when it is inconvenient or uncomfortable. You build it by telling the truth when it would be easier to hide behind silence. You build it by listening without always trying to fix what cannot be fixed in one conversation. You build it by asking better questions and giving people the time and space to share real answers. You build it by dropping your guard even when everything in you wants to armor up and protect yourself.

You have to remind yourself that your relationships are one of the most powerful yet often overlooked tools you have for your mental health. A strong and meaningful connection does not just keep your spirit alive. It can keep your body healthier, your mind clearer, and your stress levels lower. When you feel safe enough to show up as your true self and trust that someone has your back, you are better able to handle what life throws at you. Emotional safety and real connection can help you stand firm when life tests you. They remind you that you do not have to carry every burden by yourself. That is real strength.

Keep Showing Up

No matter what you have seen or what you have survived, it is never too late to build this kind of bond. You do not need the perfect moment. Start right where you are with what you have. Look around and find the relationships that matter enough to protect and grow. Have the conversations you have been putting off. Say what needs to be said, even if your voice shakes a little. Apologize when you know you have fallen short. Forgive when it frees your heart to move forward. Push yourself to open the door just a little wider than feels safe. Never forget that consistency will always matter more than big gestures that do not last.

A friendship that grows slow and steady will carry you further than one that burns bright and disappears when things get hard. Your brothers need to see you show up as your true self. Your partner needs you to share your real thoughts and feelings, not just what you think they want to hear. Your children need to see a father or an uncle or a mentor who models real emotional strength, not toughness that hides the truth. Start today. Keep showing up. This kind of closeness is worth it every single time.

Where We Go From Here

Feeling emotionally safe and securely connected to others is just as important for you now as it was when you were a child. Strong relationships are not a luxury; they are a lifeline for your mental, emotional, and physical well-being. The right connections remind you that you do not have to stand alone when life tries to knock you down. They help you stand taller and stay grounded when you face real challenges.

Connection does not grow by accident. It grows through consistent presence, real honesty, and the small, shared moments that add up over time. It grows when you trust someone enough to let them see you as you are, not just as you want to be seen. It grows stronger each time you show up when you say you will, and each time you stay when it would be easier to run. Once you become more self-aware and surround yourself with people who truly want the best for you, you can commit to the kind of growth that lasts. That commitment starts when you train yourself to adopt a growth mindset. This means believing that you can learn, change, and build new habits that shape you into the man you are working to become next.

PAUSE, REFLECT, AND RECLAIM

The need for closeness, understanding, and brotherhood is a fundamental part of who you are. Before you turn the page, examine the strength of your emotional circle. This is your chance to reclaim the bonds that build you up and reflect on what kind of teammate, friend, brother, or partner you're becoming.

Ask Yourself:

◊   Who are the people you feel safest being vulnerable with?

◊   What shared experiences have deepened your strongest bonds?

◊   How can you show up more consistently for the people who matter most?

Locker Room Wisdom:
"The final score rarely tells the whole story.
It's what happens between the plays and
your teammates that makes the team unbreakable."

PART III
COMMITMENT

This is where your vision becomes reality. After the work of self-awareness and connection, what remains is commitment, or the choice to keep moving forward with purpose. These chapters invite you to train your mind to grow through challenges, to take full ownership of your life, and to stay in the game until the win is secured. It is about discipline, focus, and the steady drive that comes from knowing why you started. You will be called to align your actions with your values, to lead with strength and humility, and to carry the ball all the way to the finish with persistence and faith.

CHAPTER 8

KEEP TRAINING
DEVELOPING A GROWTH MINDSET

Growth is not earned with one big match. It is built in the hours of drilling the same moves and the mental battle of endurance when the crowd is not there. It is forged in the early mornings, the disciplined training, and every decision to step back on the mat day after day.

Set Your Stance: Clarifying Your Values

Keep training to grow, improve your mindset, and stay fueled by your "why" no matter the cards you are dealt. When your day-to-day life lines up with what you believe in, staying motivated feels more natural. Staying in alignment is daily work. If you do not have a clear sense of what you value, take the time to look at what really matters. Common values like compassion, family, success, integrity, and faith sound good on paper. But what really keeps you going? What gets you out of bed when you are tired? Recognize and narrow your choice of values and hold them close so they can truly guide you and help you shape a life that honors them. A life that honors your values helps you step naturally into a growth mindset. But even then, it still takes deliberate effort, daily training, and a steady commitment to keep showing up. Even when your comfort zone tries to pull you back to old ways, allow your mind to lead. It is powerful when you realize your mind is your strongest muscle. It can also be your biggest barrier. The way you see the world shapes how you move in it. If you look at setbacks as permanent, they will bury you. But if you train yourself to see them as lessons, they build you up. Before we continue in this chapter, let me share another personal story.

When Coasting Becomes Costly

I was raised hearing I was smart. The adults (parents and teachers) in my life told me this, and my grades backed them up. In elementary school, I did not struggle. I excelled. As I remember, I always got the all-A honor roll every quarter. But the older I got, the more the expectations shifted. In middle school, my parents' bar stayed high enough to keep me motivated but at school, the teachers began to expect less and were satisfied with what I was giving them at the moment. In middle school, my "good enough" mindset started to grow roots. I began to turn in work late. Sometimes I did not turn it in at all with the thought of making it up later by getting a high grade on other tasks. I started settling for As and Bs even though I knew I could do better. When an occasional C showed up, neither I nor anyone else really panicked. My parents assumed a grade of that nature was simply because I was not good in that subject matter or material. The teachers did not press me to push harder and so I stayed in the middle of the pack. I was smart enough that I simply coasted by, not pushing to see what else I could do.

Don't Let Your Gift Bench Your Growth

Raw talent can win a few plays, but it's discipline that earns you a starter role. When you rely only on being "good enough," you miss the reps that sharpen your edge. Even the most gifted players still have to practice and study their film.

By the time I hit high school, my mindset had shifted from "I am good enough" to "How can I fit in?" As we explored in Chapter 5, my sense of belonging was crucial in shaping my mindset. I started to care more about blending in with others than staying true to the core values I already knew were important to me. My grades slipped from consistent As and Bs, with the occasional C, to mostly Ds and Cs. The idea of going to college did not even cross my mind very early on in high school. My parents were used to seeing good grades from me. Since there was no system that required their signature to confirm they had seen my report cards, I fell through the cracks. I never got into trouble, so my parents assumed I was still doing well. I felt like my teachers didn't expect any more from me than my elementary and middle school teachers did. It was as if they assumed I was fine staying where I was, even though my grades were not good at all. A few teachers stood out, though. I remember my English teacher, Mrs. Robinson. In tenth grade, she refused to accept a paper I turned in on time. She knew it was not my best work and as I remember it, she made me rewrite that paper three times. When I finally gave her a better version, she said, "This is the level you should be working at every single time." I did not thank her then, but I am grateful now.

Ironically, years later, I am now writing not for academic evaluation, but for a book designed to assist men, particularly Black men, in maximizing their potential in day-to-day life. In high school, my mindset was to just blend in and get by. When I reached my senior year, my mother came up with the idea that I was meant for college. She truly believed I was college material. She based this on the strong work I had done in elementary and middle school because she did not fully know where I stood academically in high school. In truth, she was not too far off because I ended up scoring higher than expected on the SAT, even though I had spent most of high school turning in work that did not reflect my real ability.

My mother started to remind me of my worth, my skills, and my true value when it came to my education. By the time I was a senior, my mindset and my actions began to line up with my real values again. When I became a college student, that mindset took root and grew stronger as I surrounded myself with people who wanted to do better and be better too. At first, my focus was fixed on success that could be proved by a piece of paper that said I had earned a degree or some kind of certification. A fixed mindset can push you to reach for things that people can see and measure. But as my own story shows, that mindset can be shaped by the environment you keep.

A growth mindset does something deeper for you as a man. It keeps you rooted in your values and does not measure your worth by trophies or praise from others. It pushes you to understand who you are at your core. It keeps your focus on the process and the progress instead of only the finish line. A growth mindset reminds you that real success is found in the way you live out your values day by day, not just in what you can hang on your wall. The man who keeps training grows stronger with every rep. The committed athlete is not just working for a trophy—he is working to see what is possible when he refuses to coast.

Mindset Check: Is It Fixed or Growing?

A fixed mindset says, "I am who I am. I have what I have. I will get what I get."

A growth mindset says, "I can improve. I can get stronger. I can learn."

When you look around your circle, who do you see? Who talks about what they are building? Who talks about what they are becoming? Who talks about how they are pushing through something hard instead of quitting?

Wrestlers with a fixed mindset avoid taking chances or shots because they're scared of missing. But growth-minded players know every miss is a lesson, not a failure. A winning season is built on missed shots, second chances, and the decision to keep wrestling or persevering until the end.

A fixed mindset locks you in a box. It keeps you afraid to fail. It tells you mistakes mean you are not good enough. A growth mindset frees you. It says mistakes are not signs you should stop but they are signs you are trying.

When you really embrace a growth mindset, you stop waiting for permission. You stop apologizing for trying again. You stop comparing your chapter one to someone else's chapter ten.

Reframe the Voice in Your Head

Training your mindset means training your self-talk. Self-talk is that constant flow of thoughts and messages that run through your mind every day. It can hype you up or drag you down. And for many of us, that voice has been shaped by years of criticism, comparison, and old beliefs. Your self-talk is like that locker room where the coach either motivates you to push harder or tears you down until you want to quit. You have to decide to become your own coach.

Just like a winning team doesn't run random plays, your mind can't operate on autopilot. Pay attention to the game and make adjustments. Paying attention to what you say to yourself is powerful because it helps build real self-esteem and real confidence. If you slow down and listen to your own mind, you will notice that your thoughts tend to repeat certain themes. If you feel strong and capable, your self-talk is usually supportive and positive. If you doubt yourself often, that stream of thoughts can be filled with fear, worry, or harsh criticism.

Reframing your mindset is about changing negative thoughts into statements that help you grow. This is not about fake positivity. This is about retraining your mental habits. Catch the negative thoughts. Name them. Reframe them. You cannot control every thought that pops up, but you can choose which thoughts you water and which you pull up by the roots.

The Power of Resilience: Get Up Again

Resilience grows through steady training and practice. It is your ability to adapt and keep moving forward when life knocks you down. Being resilient means you can pick yourself up, brush off the disappointment, take a moment to breathe, and then get back to the work that matters. Resilience is rooted in hope and optimism, but it is not just a feeling you are born with. Work at it patiently and consistently if you want to develop it.

In every sport, it's not the strongest or fastest who wins, it's the one who gets back up. Consistency is what sets growth in motion and keeps it alive. It is the daily commitment to put in focused, purposeful work that pushes you past your current limits. No shortcut or quick fix will ever replace what steady practice does for your mind and your character. When you show up for yourself every day, you become stronger and more prepared to handle whatever challenges come your way.

When you train your mind and your habits to stay consistent, you create a strong foundation for everything you want to achieve. You become someone who does not fold when pressure comes. You handle challenges with a clear mind and a steady spirit. Every time you choose to keep going, you prove to yourself that you can handle more than you once believed.

Growth Means Your Skills Can Evolve

A growth mindset reminds you that your skills and intelligence arc not locked in place. Nothing about your potential is final unless you decide to stop growing. When you believe you can improve, you give yourself permission to learn new things and stretch beyond what you were taught to expect for yourself. This mindset keeps you open to change and ready to handle new challenges.

No all-American wrestler sticks with one move forever. They watch tape, adjust their stance, and keep adding new tools to their skill set. Growth-minded men don't coast on what they learned last year, they sharpen and stretch until the new becomes second nature. Take a look at your life right now and ask yourself what you really believe about your own gifts. Do you see your talent as something that has already reached its limit, or do you see it as something you can keep building? Every skill you want to master, whether it is communication, leadership, financial knowledge, or emotional strength, can be trained. You might not have been born knowing it, but you can learn it with time and steady practice.

When you stop trying to be perfect and start focusing on steady progress, you give yourself room to fail and grow. You learn to see mistakes as lessons instead of proof that you are not good enough. Real success is not about getting everything right the first time. It lives in the choice to stand back up when you fall and keep going until you get it right.

Intrinsic Motivation: The Fuel That Lasts

External rewards do not last forever. The applause fades. The trophies collect dust on a shelf. If all you care about is the praise and recognition, you will stop putting in the work when no one is watching. Relying only on what others think of you makes your drive weak and easy to break. The man who needs constant pats on the back will struggle when the room goes quiet.

Internal motivation is what keeps you steady. When your reason for showing up is rooted in your values and vision, you do not need the world's approval to keep moving. You work because you know what it means for you, your family, and the legacy you are trying to leave behind. A growth mindset fuels this drive by helping you find purpose in the process, not just the reward. It gives you the strength to push through hard seasons and learn from the losses that come with any real journey.

When you run on internal fuel, you do not burn out when the hype disappears. You stay in it for the long haul. Your milestones feel honest and real because they match who you truly are. You learn to engage deeply with what you do, grow stronger through setbacks, and stay inspired by your own progress and by seeing others win too.

Find People Who Keep You Sharp

Iron sharpens iron. You cannot grow to your full potential in isolation. You need people in your corner who will tell you the truth, challenge your excuses, and remind you what you said you wanted when you feel tempted to settle for less. The right circle keeps you honest and focused on the bigger vision. Think about who you spend time with. Who in your circle talks about ideas instead of gossip? Who asks you the hard questions? Who pushes you to do better when you start getting too comfortable with average?

If you look around and see that your circle does not care about growing, it might be time to find new teammates. Growth does not happen in rooms where everyone is satisfied with staying the same. Connect with men who do not just talk about discipline and progress but live it out in how they lead their families, handle their money, show up at work, and give back to their communities. A good mentor can help you avoid mistakes by sharing what they learned the hard way. They can give you real game and keep you humble enough to listen when your pride tries to get in the way.

Surround yourself with people who make you a little uncomfortable in the best way. These people remind you that you always have more room to grow and more work to do. When you walk with men who see learning as a lifelong journey, you stay motivated to keep stretching beyond your comfort zone. You really do become the sum of the company you keep.

When your circle is full of people who get back up when they fail and keep looking for answers when problems show up, you start doing the same. This kind of brotherhood does more than inspire you. It pushes you to live up to your own potential.

Daily Reps Build Mastery

Growth is not something that just happens to you one day. It is a daily choice you make over and over again. Real growth is not found in a weekend workshop or a once-a-year resolution that fades by February. It shows up in the small, steady actions you take when nobody is cheering for you. Every day, you get a chance to train your mind and your habits to match the vision you say you have for your life. You train when you have a hard conversation instead of disappearing when things get uncomfortable. You train when you pick up a book instead of wasting another hour scrolling through your phone. You train when you ask for real feedback instead of pretending you already know it all. One honest choice at a time, you build trust with yourself. You grow real confidence by doing the work, not just talking about it. The man who trains daily will always outlast the man who only talks about what he could be.

When you know your reason for training, you can handle the moments when life tests you. A clear "why" keeps you moving when you feel tired, disappointed, or afraid. This is not just something to think about. This is a call for you to act. Will you let life drift by, or will you decide to take control of your own story? Will you coast when things get tough, or will you push through? Will you keep expanding on an old story that no longer fits your character, or will you write a new one that reflects the man you want to become? Growth does not come just because you want it. It comes because you show up for it every single day. It must be earned, protected, and chosen again and again.

Your reason has to be bigger than your excuses. When you know exactly why you are putting in this work, fatigue cannot stop you. Failure cannot break you. Fear cannot own you. You will get knocked down, but you will not stay there. You will hear doubt inside your own head, but you will not let it drown out your vision. You will see other men win in their own ways, but you will not waste time comparing. Instead, you will learn, you will study, and you will keep building. This is the daily work. This is what training really looks like.

Next Up: Full Ownership

The truth is simple and clear. A growth mindset is something you choose every single day. Growth is possible for every man who decides he is done drifting through life and ready to take control of where he is going. Once you choose to stop making excuses, you open the door to everything you say you want.

Building a growth mindset means you accept full responsibility for your choices, your direction, and your future. Nobody can want it for you more than you want it for yourself. Nobody can do the daily work but you. A growth mindset reminds you that you have power over what you learn, how you improve, and how you bounce back when life hits you hard. This mindset does not let you blame the world. It calls you to look in the mirror and get honest about what you will do next.

So get ready. Keep training your mind and your habits. Keep showing up for yourself. The next chapter is about what happens when you stand tall and say, "I own the wins, the losses, the lessons, and eventually, the legacy."

PAUSE, REFLECT, AND RECLAIM

Before you move on, take this time to check in with yourself. Your answers shape your next play.

Ask Yourself:

◊ When was the last time you chose growth over comfort? What was the result?

◊ Who is in your circle that challenges you to grow?

◊ What does it look like for you to show up and train daily?

Locker Room Wisdom:
"Growth is not a finish line.
The man who keeps training
becomes the one who is always ready."

CHAPTER 9

OWNING THE BALL

TAKING RESPONSIBILITY FOR YOUR LIFE

Back in 2018, I stumbled across this new world called podcasting while I was preparing for my state licensing exam. At that time, I studied the way many of us in Generation X were taught. I flipped through paid study guides and read prep books cover to cover. I highlighted pages and worked my way through endless notes. But I also started exploring free resources in videos on YouTube and listening to podcasts on my phone. I started soaking up knowledge without even realizing how much it was changing me. Those free resources opened my eyes to how much valuable knowledge can and should be easier to find and understand for anyone who is searching for it.

That's when an idea sparked: maybe I could use podcasting to talk about mental health in a real and relatable way. At first, I tried to get on other people's shows. I sent emails, DMs, and pitched myself but nothing landed. It would have been easy to blame gatekeepers for not giving me a shot, but sitting around waiting didn't make sense. I was blessed to meet a young man from a local university who was in his senior year studying mass communication. He needed an internship to complete his degree, and I needed help launching a show. I told him, "Help me get this podcast off the ground, and you will earn your internship hours." That's how the podcast Speaking with Gravity was launched in the fall of 2020.

The truth is, blaming others for not opening a door for you won't move you forward. Real growth happens when you own what you want to do, love it enough to bet on yourself, and find a way to make it real. I could have kept waiting for an invitation but instead, I created my own. And funny enough, once I did, invitations started coming my way. Today, I have been invited as a guest on multiple platforms and my own show has reached thousands of people who needed to hear the message I carry. When the game is on the line, you won't always be in the perfect position. A lot of men sit on the sidelines waiting for the perfect moment. Waiting for the perfect partner, the perfect job, the perfect break. But life rarely hands out perfect moments. When the ball is in your hands, you must take full responsibility for your decision. Whether you choose to pass or shoot, be confident and clear about your move because the next step is yours alone. Whatever you decide, be sure you know exactly how to follow through.

Take the Blame Off Others, Put the Power Back in Your Hands

Let's be honest. Blaming others feels good for a moment. It gives you a quick sense of relief. If you can blame your boss or even the weight of systemic oppression, you might convince yourself that you are not the problem. You can point to police brutality, lack of access to capital, minimal networking opportunities, or being a product of your environment as reasons for where you are. But blaming never moves the ball forward. It never helps you score.

Like a team that keeps blaming the refs for every loss, you'll never improve if you refuse to face the truth. Real responsibility means looking in the mirror first. It means asking yourself, What can I control right now? What move can I make next? This question is powerful because it reminds you that although you cannot change the entire game, you control your next play. You control whether you pass, shoot, or dribble with purpose.

When you take responsibility for where you stand on the court, you unlock the possibility of your next play. This does not mean you excuse the rules of the game or the unfair referees. It does not mean ignoring the systemic barriers designed to hold you back. Instead, it means refusing to hand over the ball to anyone else. You keep the ball in your hands. You own your moves. That is how you begin to change the score of your life.

Maturity Means Owning It All – The Good and the Bad

It is easy to own the wins. We have no problem telling people about the promotion we earned, the new car we drive, the degree we finished, or the highlights we want replayed. The real test of maturity shows up when you own the losses with the same honesty and courage.

Think about the game for a second. Have you ever seen a player miss an open shot and then point at a teammate? Maybe he dropped the pass because he felt it was not thrown in the right spot. Maybe he turned the ball over but blamed his teammate for not looking for the ball. We have all seen that player who refuses to own his part. You can spot it the moment it happens. He does not want the mistake added to his stat sheet. But the players who lead any team are different. They stand up in front of everyone and own what went wrong. They do not blame the referee or the bad floor or the noise in the crowd. They look their teammates in the eye and say, "My bad. I'll get it back."

You need that same mindset when you step off the court and handle your own life. You become a man people trust when you can admit you missed a shot. Maybe you dropped the ball with your family. Maybe you fumbled your money or your career plans. Maybe the environment you came from made it harder to even get in the game. Maybe you have faced police harassment or no capital to start with. All of that is real. But when you stand in front of the mirror and say, "I knew what it was, that was on me too. I'll get it back," you keep your power.

People can count on you when they know your word means something. You do not hide behind excuses or blame the crowd when the shot does not fall. You own the game, every quarter and every minute, no matter if it results in a win or a loss. That is how you become the player everybody wants on their team.

Integrity Starts With You

We often say integrity is about being honest with other people. That sounds good and looks good on paper. But the truth that many men do not want to face is that real integrity begins when you stop lying to yourself.

Think about how you show up in your own game. Are you telling yourself you are putting in work when you know you are jogging through practice? Are you telling yourself you are serious about changing your life when you cannot sit down, create a plan, and stick to it for even one week? Are you calling yourself a leader when you cannot lead in your own home by managing your daily habits? Taking responsibility and exhibiting integrity is not just a one-time decision. It is a daily practice. Every day, you wake up with a debt to yourself and to the people who trust you.

If you are real with yourself, you already know where you have been cutting corners. You know the workouts you skipped when it came to being vulnerable, building real emotional closeness, and taking time to understand your true values instead of chasing your accolades. You know when you are just throwing up shots to pad your stats instead of sticking to the game plan that helps you win for real. Nobody else needs to know every detail, but you do. Growth only happens when you stop pretending.

Integrity means your actions match your words and your words match what you really want. It means you do not show off your highlight reel on social media while your real life stays stuck behind the scenes. When you stop lying to yourself, you free up energy to make real plays that change the scoreboard for you and the people counting on you.

Curveballs Happen – Your Response Shapes Your Story

Life will test you in ways you did not plan for. You might lose a job you thought was safe. You might carry the weight of setbacks that blindside you when you are already tired of fighting. One of the hardest and most unfair blows is disproportionate incarceration amongst Black men. Sometimes the charge is minor but the time is major. Sometimes the system gives you a record that follows you long after you walk out. That record can bench you from the job you want and the chance to provide for your family.

To be clear, this is real. It is not in your imagination. But what happens next is not only about what has been done to you. It is about how you respond when the ball is back in your hands. Do you stand still and blame the system forever or do you counter with a new play? Do you pass the ball and single out a specific player or do you utilize all five positions? Maybe you cannot break into finance or healthcare because of that record. But are you willing to pivot and train as a barber, a welder, or an HVAC technician so you can still score? Your response is everything. Response is part of the game plan that turns broken plays into breakthrough moments.

Response is the difference between being stopped at the three-point line and finding a lane for the two instead. Response means you stay ready to learn. You might need to get help from mentors who can show you how to expunge a charge. You might need to build new skills that make you valuable to a specific industry.

Setbacks are real but they do not have to be your final score. When you look back at what tried to break you, ask yourself what it taught you. Ask what new skills you picked up. Ask who you became because you refused to sit on the sideline. That is how pain turns into power.

The Discipline of Choosing What You Want Most

Responsibility and discipline go together like a strong point guard and a reliable big man. It is one thing to talk about wanting more for your life. It is another thing to put in the work and sacrifice for it when nobody is watching. Real discipline means you choose what you want most over what feels good in the moment. You owe it to yourself to guard your vision. You owe it to your family to keep showing up strong and steady. You owe it to your community to use your gifts in ways that lift more than just you. When you see responsibility and discipline this way, they stop feeling like a burden and start feeling like your foundation.

If you want a healthy body, you cannot keep eating junk food every night just because it hits the spot right now. If you want financial freedom, you cannot spend every dollar the moment it hits your account just because it feels good for a moment. If you want a relationship that lasts, you cannot disappear when things get tense just because conflict makes you uncomfortable. Growth costs something up front but pays you back later.

Deferred gratification or learning to wait is part of real maturity. Telling yourself "not yet" is not punishment. It is protection for what matters most. When you master this, you stop falling for quick fixes and cheap highs that drain your focus. You build habits that match the future you say you want. Every good team has a system that works. The same is true for your life when you stay disciplined enough to run your plays the right way.

You Are the Common Denominator

If every job you work feels toxic, take a hard look at how you show up when you clock in. If every relationship ends the same way, ask yourself what patterns you keep repeating even when you know better. If every goal slips through your fingers, study your level of commitment, your follow-through, and your willingness to keep pushing when things get uncomfortable.

This is not about shame or beating yourself up. This is about having real clarity. Once you accept that you are the common link between every area of your life, you stop searching for scapegoats. You get honest about your part. You get serious about your choices and what they cost you.

You do not get to control everything that life throws your way, but you do control how you prepare, how you respond, and how you adjust your game plan for the next round. That alone makes you powerful. It keeps the ball in your hands no matter what defense life puts in front of you.

Stop Waiting – Start Creating

Stop waiting for permission to move forward. Stop waiting for someone to tap you on the shoulder and say it is your turn. Start where you are and use what you already have in your hands. Build as you go and trust that you will figure out the rest while you are in motion. If you want to write, pick up the pen and write. If you want to lead, step forward and lead. If you want to change, do it today. Nobody is coming to save you or hand you the perfect setup. You are the rescue plan you have been hoping for all this time.

Owning your life means you become your own coach and your own motivator. You hold yourself accountable for the life you say you want. You build your own system one decision at a time. You create your own openings that nobody else can block. When the big doors open, you will be ready because you put in the practice long before the crowd showed up. Real freedom comes when you stop blaming others and stand firm in your own choices. You do not have to be perfect, but you do have to be honest. Every day you get to decide whether your actions pull you closer to the man you want to be or push you further away. When you own those choices, you live on purpose, move with intention, and leave excuses behind because you do not need them anymore.

The Next Play: Staying Committed

As you claim ownership, you set yourself up for success by staying the course no matter what comes your way. Commitment to your daily choices evolves into a steady lifestyle. The discipline keeps you focused through all four quarters of life's game, even when the score is not in your favor.

So the question is simple and direct. When the ball is in your hands, what will you do with it? Will you hold it and freeze up, or will you take your shot and trust your preparation? The choice is yours every single time.

PAUSE, REFLECT, AND RECLAIM

As you close this chapter, take a moment to reset. These questions are designed to move you from reaction to responsibility, from excuses to execution. Your accountability is your advantage.

Ask Yourself:

◊ Where in your life have you been waiting instead of creating?

◊ What excuses do you use that keep you from fully owning your next move?

◊ How are you training for the life you say you want, not just talking about it?

Locker Room Wisdom:
"You can't always control the score,
but you can control your commitment."

CHAPTER 10

PLAYING THE LONG GAME

STAYING COMMITTED

Playing the Long Game – Staying Committed to the Win

Too many of us learn to settle for a win today with less care for tomorrow and the remainder of the season or the remainder of our life. Many of us grew up facing real barriers that can make simply staying in the game feel impossible. Maybe your father was never there to pass you the ball or teach you how to navigate life. Maybe you grew up without strong men around you to show you what love, respect, kindness, composure, appreciation, discipline, and responsibility really look like. For some of us, the home-field advantage was not so much of an advantage. The lack of a nuclear family felt more like scattered teammates with one coach or GM to bring it all together. Add to that the weight of wounds passed down from elders and generations before who never had a real chance to heal. It is no wonder that we learn to chase the single wins instead of building up our endurance for the whole season.

A man who builds something that lasts will also have the discipline to keep showing up, even when nobody is watching. He does not leave the field when the first play gets shut down. He does not fold when the cheering stops. He does not quit when life's defense hits him hard. He lines up for the next down. He studies the playbook. He trusts that his quiet and valiant efforts will lead to touchdowns not only in this game but others to come. You probably know a few men who chase highlight reels instead. They celebrate every small gain like they won the Super Bowl but forget to show up for the next game. The truth is: when you live only for accolades, you stay addicted to external validation and forget about what is real. But the man playing the long game keeps his eyes on the whole season, not just the scoreboard today. He understands that every practice, every rep, every block, and every hard lesson is part of building his legacy. When you know this, you do not just play to win a game, but you play to win your life.

Stop Needing Immediate and Frequent Validation

Earlier in this book, we talked about the value of deferred gratification, which is also called delayed gratification. Some people misunderstand this principle and think it means you must sacrifice your happiness today so you can be happy tomorrow. But as Brian Tracy explained, the ability to discipline yourself to delay gratification in the short term so you can enjoy greater rewards in the long term is an essential requirement for true success. One of the first signs that you are self-determined is that you stop needing someone else to pat you on the back every other day just to keep going.

Without realizing it, you might deal with something called delay discounting. This means rewards feel less valuable the further away they are in the future. Some people discount these future rewards more than others. Imagine someone offers you twenty dollars right now or one hundred dollars a year from now. Many people would choose the smaller amount today rather than wait for the larger reward later. You have to ask yourself an honest question: Do I lean toward wanting quick rewards so much that I overlook how much better it would be to plan for greater rewards down the road?

Getting quick validation feels good in the moment. It is like sugar: sweet for a minute but not good for your body when you keep chasing it. When you live only for what feels good right now, you will twist your vision to please people and get praise in the moment. You may even start watering down your real purpose just to get a few more likes and quick applause. When you choose to play the long game, you tell yourself the truth. You say that your work matters even if nobody sees it today. You trust that what you are planting now will grow into real fruit later.

There have been moments when I seriously thought about giving up this current path and choosing an easier road. I could work for someone else, collect a steady paycheck, and use that money to make sure my children have what they need. But if I simply trade my time for money, I would be giving them things while neglecting to give them me. On my days off, worn out from work, I would spend my time unwinding in my hobbies and reliving old glory days with the college crew instead of truly connecting with my wife and my kids. I could choose that path, or I could choose the harder one, the path of deferred gratification.

I have yet to win any big awards or earn the kind of public recognition that society loves to celebrate. But every birthday, every holiday, every Father's Day, every major milestone, and every unexpected conversation with my wife, my children, or a local citizen reminds me of the real rewards. I see the proof in their eyes and hear it in their words: I have shown up for them. By answering my calling to be a therapist and spreading awareness about mental health, I have shown up for my family and my community. I traded quick validation for something that lasts far longer and that is legacy.

Your Vision Needs Clarity and Flexibility

A man without a vision is like a tailback running full speed and avoiding tackles but not heading downfield toward the end zone. He is moving. He is putting in the work. He is breaking a sweat every day. But when the play is finally over, he is not where he truly wants to be. Your vision must be clear enough to keep you focused but open enough to expand as you grow. If your vision is too shaded, you will keep hopping from one idea to the next and lose your drive when the game gets tough. If your vision is too blurry, the first time life sends pressure your way, you will fold because you have no room to adjust the plan.

Go back to your core values and ask yourself honestly, "What am I really building here and why does it matter?" Be real about what you truly want. If you want to build a business, do not just launch any business for the sake of saying you are an owner. Build something connected to what you love and enjoy so that it feeds your family, creates jobs for people in your community, and tackles real problems people face every day. Now your vision has depth and roots strong enough to keep you steady when the storms come.

A clear vision will guide you back in the right direction every time you feel lost or worn down. A flexible vision will help you adjust your game plan when the old one stops working. Think about it like this. Would you tell a wide receiver to run his route toward the first down marker and then expect him to stay stuck when the defender locks him up? If he does not know how to adjust his route, he will run hard but still come up short of the first down. He might look the part, but he will not move the chains forward. When you know how to stay clear and stay flexible, you keep the drive alive no matter what the defense throws your way.

Too many men say yes to big dreams but never take the time to define the mission, the plan, or the real cost. You might say you want to be successful but never write down what success actually means for you, and without that, your vision stays cloudy. You must be clear about what better looks like for you and then make choices every day that prove you mean it. If you do not have a clear vision or target, then you are wasting energy even if you show up committed every day. Do not just commit to staying busy, hustling, and working hard. Commit to a vision that helps you work wisely. Commit to a plan that matches the man you are growing into. Put in the work with strategy, with clear direction, and with a purpose that lines up with the man you want to see when you look in the mirror.

Build an Environment That Mirrors Your Future

Your environment shapes you more than you think. For the sake of this passage, think of your environment as the people connected to you. If your space is built for comfort only, you will keep getting the same easy results. Seeking support from others—whether it is friends, family, or a mentor—helps you stay accountable and motivated. But if your circle is full of people who tap out when life gets hard, you will find yourself lowering your standards to match theirs.

If you want legacy and not just wins, you must build an environment that reflects your future, not your past. Never underestimate how powerful the right support system can be for getting you unstuck. Think about a wrestler stepping onto the mat. Although he appears to be alone and mano a mano, he does not step on alone. He has a coach in his corner, teammates in the stands, and someone recording film so he can break down what he did right and what he needs to fix. The right support system works the same way for you. When you are tired, the right people remind you that you do not have to fight alone. When your confidence takes a hit, your circle reminds you why you got on the mat in the first place. Additional eyes on your situation can reveal solutions or opportunities you might have missed on your own.

So how do you build that kind of circle? Start by looking at what you already have. Lean on the friends who keep it real with you, the family members who tell you the truth, or that one coworker who wants to see you win. If you need more, expand your circle. Join groups or spaces where men push each other to level up. Find a local network for your field, a mastermind group, or an alumni circle that connects you with others who know the fight you are in. If you cannot find that support where you arc, do not bc afraid to bring in professional help. Get a coach for your business plan, a mentor who has walked the road ahead of you, or a therapist who can help you untangle what keeps you from stepping fully into who you say you want to be.

To find the right resources, be clear about what you need. Maybe you need accountability to stick with your goals the same way a wrestler needs a training partner to show up for practice every day. Maybe you need motivation when life tries to pin you down. Maybe you need someone to help you see the habits that keep tripping you up match after match. Be honest about what keeps you stuck and be open about what it will take to break free.

Once you've determined what you need, look around you. Everything you see is either helping you or hurting you. No one navigates life's challenges alone and a strong support system is essential for clarity, motivation, and momentum. Just think of the team behind Bubba Wallace, the NASCAR driver who broke barriers by winning at Talladega. He did not get there alone. He needed a team in the pits, a crew chief, and people who believed in his vision. Without that team, crossing that finish line would have been impossible. You do not have to move to another city or cut off every friend you have known since childhood to create the perfect environment. But you do have to be real about what helps you grow and what keeps you stuck. You and your circle can build a plan together that helps you step back into whatever space you are in, stronger than you were the day before. Reach out to someone in your network or begin exploring professional options today so you can reach yours as well.

Your Lasting Legacy

The long game is all about staying persistent for a reason that matters. Some men keep working hard but waste their effort holding on to old habits that do not help them grow. Purpose gives your effort direction. It keeps you steady when life tests you and storms try to knock you off track.

As you build something worth keeping, you will see that real success is not about quick rewards but about the legacy you leave behind. Your legacy is built one day at a time. Every experience you have had since childhood shapes how you see the world today. What you hold onto from those memories shows what you value and who you want to become. Over time you will start to notice patterns in how you live and think. If you see patterns that keep you stuck, you can change them through learning, honest reflection, and help from people who want to see you win.

To keep moving forward, stay consistent and clear about where you are headed. Real progress comes when you make choices on purpose and build connections with people who remind you who you are. Real belonging happens when you have people who see the real you and still choose you. Every man wants to feel like he matters. When you know your role and keep showing up, you learn that your worth is not about being the best but about being dependable and trustworthy. When you know who you are and surround yourself with the right people, you stay ready to grow every day.

In the end, the choice is yours alone. The ball is in your hands. You decide how you play this game. Long-term success belongs to the man who keeps showing up with discipline, vision, and steady effort. Stay in the game. Keep building what lasts. That is how you win for real.

PAUSE, REFLECT, AND RECLAIM

The long game is won by vision, strategy, and endurance. Legacy is where perseverance and preparation meets purpose.

Ask Yourself:

◊ What are you doing today that builds toward the future you say you want?

◊ What distractions keep pulling you off your path, and why are you still letting them?

◊ Who in your circle holds you accountable when you lose focus?

Locker Room Wisdom:
"Hall of Fame careers aren't gained in one season.
They are won in how you show up for each practice, each play,
and each game. The long game rewards the man who refuses to quit."

CONCLUSION
THE FINAL PLAY

This book found its way to you for a reason. Maybe a therapist suggested it. Maybe you heard about it from a friend or stumbled across it through some form of media. Or maybe you simply knew you needed better offensive strategies and defensive alignments to navigate this game of life. You stayed with it from the first page to the last because something in you wanted more. Perhaps you desired plays to help you lead better, love deeper, or ensure you are developing the legacy you want for yourself. Through each chapter, you revisited experiences from childhood to adulthood and explored how those experiences shaped your view of yourself and the world around you. You have seen how your identity is built each day through the choices you make as you keep learning what matters most to you and how you want to live. This book is not a guarantee of an undefeated season or a quick fix to turn around your season. It is a reminder that growth is about steady progress, not perfection. It is about building a life that aligns with your values and the man you want to be.

I still remember the summer of 2007 when I stood in a hospital room, moving back and forth between my newborn under the warming light and my wife recovering in the next room. In that moment, I knew my life would never be the same. My life was no longer just mine but it was ours as a family. Every play called would echo through the lives of my children, my wife, and my community. I knew I had a solid foundation thanks to how I was raised, but I also knew I had to keep growing. I needed therapy, mentors, and faith to guide me. My game plan became a commitment to keep learning and becoming better.

In many ways, this book is here to help you develop your own game plan. Take what you have learned and use it to play the long game. Let the parts that challenged you push you toward more growth. Seek out counseling, community, and mentorship for deeper insight. But for the insight you do have, what will you do with it? Knowledge without action changes nothing. Insight without practice is just theory. Real change is what you choose to do next.

Your story is not over. Your legacy is being written one choice, one habit, and one play at a time. Keep training your mind, aligning your goals with your values, and building habits that reflect the man you say you want to be. Everything you've read, everything you've reflected on can be a tool to create your new playbook.

ACKNOWLEDGMENT

First and foremost, I give all glory and honor to God. Without His presence, guidance, and patience with me through the highs and lows of this journey and my life, this book would not exist. He called me to this assignment, walked with me along the way, and positioned the right people at every step. This offering is for His glory.

To my wife, Malinda—thank you for being my anchor. Your patience and quiet faith in me have propelled me in ways you cannot imagine. I love you deeply and I honor you as my wife and the mother of my children.

To my children—Destyn, Peyton, Sydney, and Bailey—thank you for being you. Being blessed to be your father and given the task to coach you in life has empowered me in ways I could not have imagined without your presence. This book stands as another example that you can do anything you set your mind to.

To my mom, Gloria, and my dad, Clarence—I stand here today because of your prayers, the example you lived, the sacrifices you made, and the home you created for me and my siblings.

To my siblings—Rico, Tiffany, and Taylor—thank you for your encouragement and for cheering me on, even when you didn't know I was down.

To my nieces and nephews—I hope I made you proud.

Jabber, Marquise, and Robbie—your conversations and inquisitive nature gave me fuel to produce this work. I saw the need for this message because of you, and I also stayed the course because of you.

To Reea Rodney—my publishing consultant and book coach—thank you for seeing the bigger vision and holding space for me to grow into it. Your patience, encouragement, and expertise elevated this project far beyond what I imagined. You challenged me to go deeper while still honoring my authentic voice, and for that, I'm grateful.

To the Dara Publishing team, thank you for taking this message and treating it like your own. From coordination to coaching, layout to formatting, for creating a cover that speaks boldly before a single word is read. You captured the spirit of the work with precision. Your professionalism and support ensured this book would not just be released, but released well.

To the readers—especially the men—who will pick up this book with open hearts and a desire to grow: thank you. You are not alone. This book was written with you in mind, and my deepest hope is that you find language for what you've been feeling and a roadmap for where you're going.

Finally, to every friend, supporter, colleague, mentor, and educator who has poured into my journey—thank you. Some names may not appear on this page, but your impact is printed into the very spirit of this book.

May this work serve as proof that your love, investment, and prayers were never wasted.

With gratitude,

Kervin K. Searles, LPC

ABOUT THE AUTHOR

Kervin Searles is a Licensed Professional Counselor, speaker, and mental health advocate dedicated to helping men live with clarity and purpose. With over a decade of experience, he has guided countless individuals through trauma, major life transitions, and the challenging work of breaking generational cycles to build healthier, more meaningful relationships.

Kervin holds a Bachelor of Arts in Psychology from Anderson University and a Masters in Counseling Psychology from Troy University. He is part owner of **Gravity Counseling Group**, a practice that blends clinical expertise with real-life strategies to empower individuals to heal without shame and embrace strength through vulnerability.

Outside the therapy room, Kervin is a keynote speaker, facilitates workshops, leads community programs, and produces Speaking with Gravity—a podcast that normalizes open, practical conversations about mental health. He is deeply committed to creating spaces where Black men feel seen, heard, and equipped to grow.

When he's not counseling, Kervin enjoys spending time with his wife and four children, mentoring youth, watching sports, and staying involved in faith-based community initiatives that uplift and inspire others.

Kervin believes every man deserves the chance to heal, grow, and build a life rooted in truth, trust, and love.

Connect with Kervin:
Website: www.gravitycounselinggroup.com
Instagram: @gravitycounselinggroup
Facebook: Gravity Counseling Group
Podcast: Speaking with Gravity
Email: admin@gravitycounselinggroup.com

Thank You for Reading My Book

Thank you for journeying through the pages of Undrafted & Purposed. I wrote this book with men like you in mind— men who desire more for themselves, their families, and their communities. This is more than a book; it is a guide to understanding yourself in a deeper way and reshaping how you see the world.

My hope is that the tools, stories, and wisdom here have given you language for your experiences, courage to face your truth, and a renewed commitment to show up—not just in pursuit of making it big, but in living big in the league called LIFE.

If this book impacted you, encouraged you, or gave you something to think about, I would love to hear from you.

Please take a moment to leave a review on Amazon. Your feedback helps other readers discover the book and encourages me to continue creating tools for growth and healing.

www.ingramcontent.com/pod-product-compliance
Lightning Source LLC
Chambersburg PA
CBHW060642130626
46555CB00002B/921